BUILDING EFFECTIVE AFTERSCHOOL PROGRAMS

This book is dedicated to the memory of

Mr. John H. Hollifield

Sir John, thank you for all of your kindness
and the support that you showed me
during the short time that I knew you.
This book is definitely a product of your work.

BUILDING EFFECTIVE AFTERSCHOOL PROGRAMS

OLATOKUNBO S. FASHOLA

Foreword by Robert E. Slavin

CORWIN PRESS, INC.
A Sage Publications Company
Thousand Oaks, California

For information:

Corwin Press, Inc.
A Sage Publications Company
2455 Teller Road
Thousand Oaks, California 91320
E-mail: order@corwinpress.com

Sage Publications Ltd.
6 Bonhill Street
London EC2A 4PU
United Kingdom

Sage Publications India Pvt. Ltd.
M-32 Market
Greater Kailash I
New Delhi 110 048 India

Printed in the United States of America

Library of Congress Cataloging-in-Publication Data

Fashola, Olatokunbo S.
    Building effective afterschool programs / by Olatokunbo S. Fashola.
        p. cm.
    Includes bibliographical references and index.
    ISBN 0-7619-7877-1 (cloth) — ISBN 0-7619-7878-X (pbk.)
    1. Student activities—United States. 2. Students—Services for—United States. 3. Mentoring in education—United States.
4. Compensatory education—United States.   I. Title.
    LB3605 .F37 2001
    371.8'9'0973—dc21   2001001654

This book is printed on acid-free paper.

02 03 04 05 06 07 7 6 5 4 3 2

Acquiring Editor: Robb Clouse
Associate Editor: Kylee Liegl
Corwin Editorial Assistant: Erin Buchanan
Production Editor: Olivia Weber
Editorial Assistant: Ester Marcelino
Typesetter/Designer: Larry Bramble
Indexer: Teri Greenberg
Cover Designer: Michael Dubowe

Contents

Foreword

There is never a shortage of good ideas in education. Our problem is that good ideas are so often misapplied.

In recent years, the idea of extending the school day has become popular throughout the United States. The potential of an extended day is clear. Afterschool programs can provide additional time for learning of basic skills and enrichment opportunities tailored to children's individual interests. They can provide cultural programs, sports, drama, and community service opportunities. They can engage students in productive, prosocial activities as an alternative to unstructured, unsupervised time that many children with working parents may put to ill use, be it in passive television watching or delinquent activities.

The problem of the afterschool movement, in fact, is in the very breadth of its potential outcomes. All too often, extended-day programs expected to increase basic skills end up instead as enrichment at best, babysitting at worst. Afterschool programs may be funded to help children who are at risk of school failure but then are attended by the children who are not at risk. In a time of increasing accountability based on test performance, in which children may be retained in grade if they do not achieve at acceptable levels, afterschool and summer school programs are often proposed as a means of giving children a second chance to make up lost ground. If they fail to do so, children suffer, and the programs themselves are deemed failures. In such circumstances, providing services that are not focused on academic achievement may cause real damage to vulnerable children. Alternatively, an afterschool program designed to serve the whole child, to provide cultural and intellectual enrichment, would be considered a failure if it instead focused on academic basics. Yet these mismatches between intentions and actions frequently occur in afterschool programs expected to serve many masters.

This book presents a sensible, comprehensive overview of afterschool programs and, in particular, reviews research on programs that have been or could be used in afterschool programs to increase academic achievement. The book begins with the perception that the afterschool movement, represented most dramatically by the substantial funding provided to the federal 21st Century Learning Communities program, creates an extraordinary opportunity for America's children. Its purpose is to give readers an overview of research and best practices to enable them to make intelligent choices, to match the objectives of afterschool programs with strategies capable of achieving those objectives. In this, it provides a unique source of information, experience, and evidence that is essential for any educator or policymaker involved in planning afterschool programs for children.

—Robert E. Slavin
Johns Hopkins University

Preface

The concern about what takes place during the nonschool hours, especially when there is no direct supervision of children, has led to the creation and development of many afterschool initiatives. The reasons behind the surge of interest in afterschool programs have to do with the culmination of many different factors. With welfare reform, the number of working mothers, double-parent families needing supervision of children, single-parent families, and violence in communities, low academic performance and juvenile delinquency in general have increased. Families, political parties, and communities are coming together to address a critical need for afterschool supervision of school-age children (Mott Foundation, 1999). This issue is indisputable, and everyone agrees that there is a need. A big question, however, is what to do during the nonschool hours and how to do it.

The 21st Century Community Learning Centers (21st CCLCs) are the most publicized federal initiative created for afterschool and summer school in a long time. The 21st CCLCs were created to provide safe and enriching environments for school-age children during the nonschool hours. They were conceived in an attempt to provide enhanced learning opportunities in a safe, drug-free environment for children during the nonschool hours, but the one stipulation was that the centers had to be housed in school buildings (de Kanter, Pederson, & Bobo, 1997). In a joint effort between the U.S. Department of Education and the Mott Foundation, money was made available to establish afterschool programs around the country in 1997, and 3 years later this effort is still being funded.

This book was conceived about 5 years ago after having several discussions with administrators, policymakers, principals, teachers, and researchers involved in afterschool programs. The administrators were applying for funding, policymakers were providing funding, the principals and teachers were receiving funding, and all were wondering what to do with it. Researchers were wondering, "What works?" Actually, this was the basic question on the minds of all the aforementioned stakeholders.

However, in the attempt to answer this question, it became clear that there was no simple answer. Before being able to answer the question about what works during the afterschool hours, it was important to investigate issues such as the needs and goals of the program, the goals and expectations of the funders, the services provided in the various settings, the populations being served, the obstacles to implementation, and a combination of all these. The answer to the question "What works?" evolved from a few phrases to sentences, paragraphs, chapters, and eventually, this book. Investigating these questions was just the first step. Beyond this book, my ultimate goal as a researcher is to investigate afterschool programs that show either evidence of promise or evidence of effectiveness during the nonschool hours. Thus when I began my search, I asked various types of programs to provide program descriptions and evidence of effectiveness. From the program descriptions, it became evident that although there were numerous programs around the country, many had similar functions and structures, served similar populations, and had similar goals and intentions. However, they had varying evidence of promise or effectiveness. This book is structured so that if readers have specific questions about how to use afterschool programs, the titles of the chapters will lead them to the programs that will best benefit the needs of the population in question.

Overview of the Book

The first chapter details the steps taken to find and select programs reviewed in the book, provides a brief overview of the various programs, and presents the standards for determining whether a program is categorized as effective or promising. Finally, it explains the term *evidence of effectiveness* and encourages readers to structure the evaluation of their programs so that they are ultimately able to provide this information.

The second chapter explores language arts programs that have been, or could be, used during the afterschool hours. Over the past few years, a lot of emphasis has been placed on reading and writing during the school hours. There have been several debates in the field of literacy as to which approach is best suited for teaching reading. Rather than engage in a debate about phonics versus whole language, it is more practical to understand what concepts and skills are essential to developing as a fully equipped good reader. Phonemic segmentation, orthographic awareness, metacognitive skills, comprehension skills, and graphophonemic awareness (awareness of the relationship between graphemes and phonemes) are all equally important components of the reading process. It is valuable to focus on programs that have some or all of these components and how they can be used to effectively improve weak reading skills. To get the most out of the program, the instructors should find the areas in which their students or the current reading packages are lacking or weak and implement these programs in conjunction with the programs currently being used. For example, if a program does not teach comprehension skills, the instructors might decide to use a program that focuses specifically on this skill in its afterschool reading component that also teaches comprehension skills to complement the decoding, writing or other skills being taught. Chapter 2 does not select one program over another but, rather, encourages the reader to select the program that best suits the needs of the students and teachers in the afterschool program.

The third chapter addresses academically oriented, enrichment, afterschool programs. These programs are unique in that they cover areas beyond the basics and tend to be nonremedial. These programs can be used to enrich students in the areas of science, reading, mathematics, and social studies. The programs covered in this chapter did not necessarily originate in universities or school settings. Rather, they were developed externally either by for-profit or not-for-profit organizations.

As of now, none of these programs has solid evidence of effectiveness, but they are included in this book because they are widely used, and some of the programs are undergoing preliminary evaluations. School-based afterschool programs intending to adopt these programs might find this chapter and Chapter 7 on evaluation particularly helpful.

The fourth chapter addresses tutoring programs. This chapter differs from others in that it specifically addresses volunteer tutoring programs, with the exception of Project IMPACT, which is a study skills program. This chapter was added because many programs receiving afterschool funding often find themselves underfunded and understaffed. They are usually in need of additional instructors or tutors, to reduce the student-to-teacher ratio, and cannot always afford to pay the stipends that should be paid to credentialed teachers. Some programs choose to hire well-intentioned volunteers, who are willing to perform the duties of tutors with minimal pay. Although this idea may seem noble, programs must be careful, because good intentions do not always lead to good outcomes. In fact, Wasik (1997) showed that very few volunteer tutoring programs have solid evidence of effectiveness. This does not mean that programs should not consider using volunteer tutors but, rather, that they should train them and ensure that they are able to provide effective services. The chapters on creating an effective afterschool program and on evaluation address this topic. Some of the programs in Chapter 4, such as Howard Street Tutoring Program, are comprehensive programs, and others, such as Reading Recovery, focus on individual skills.

The fifth chapter addresses community-based afterschool programs. Some of the most widely known and funded programs, such as the New York City Beacons program and the Los Angeles's Better Educated Students for Tomorrow (LA's BEST), are community-based programs housed in schools. Such programs have social, community, and academic goals and components as a part of their main infrastructure. For newer programs attempting to follow in the footsteps of some of these already established programs, Chapter 5 provides a brief description of these components and evidence of evaluation or effectiveness.

Chapter 5 also addresses community-based afterschool programs such as Boy Scouts and Girl Scouts, Camp Fire Boys and Girls, and Boys & Girls Clubs of America. These programs are included because, although many afterschool programs may have academic foci, the chapter on building effective afterschool programs addresses the relevance of additional components of afterschool programs, such as recreational, cultural, and character development programs. For schools seeking additional components to add to their programs, this chapter provides some information on additional programs that could provide services to the students and their families beyond academics during the school year.

Chapter 6 was written as a result of several requests from principals, administrators, teachers, and the publishers. The main topic of concern was "How do we create an afterschool program now that we have the money?" However, the creation and planning of afterschool programs begins long before the program receives funding. In other words, if programs wait until after they have received funding to begin to plan and create the program, then they will end up having to play catch-up. This chapter begins with the needs assessment and ends with the effects of the various types of programs on children. School-based programs intending to create afterschool programs should use this chapter as a resource and also especially examine the section on training, obstacles to success, and the importance of creating the various components.

The seventh chapter addresses the topic of evaluation, which harks back to the basic question that fueled this book: What works? The initial literature search disclosed that there were few programs with evidence of effectiveness during the afterschool hours, and thus the mission to broaden the search began. One of the constant threads across the various studies was that although the programs may have undergone evaluation, the evaluation designs were not rigorous. The goal of Chapter 7 is to guide afterschool-funding recipients as to how to conduct evaluations of their programs. This chapter covers the relevance of evaluation, different types of evaluation, various design models, and, finally, the limitations of program evaluation. The chapter concludes by encouraging readers to use the best components of evaluation that will complement and ultimately improve their programs.

The eighth and concluding chapter discusses the factors that make afterschool programs successful. Components such as specific goals, professional development, training, and evaluation are identified. This chapter also addresses barriers to participation in afterschool programs, with the most frequent barriers being transportation, cost, and, sometimes, responsibility for siblings.

Chapter 8 revisits the topic of what works and challenges readers to discover what works for their programs. In actuality, there is no single program that will address the needs of every community, but there are some underlying components such as planning, training, evaluation, structure, and content that are critical factors for success, regardless of the goals of the afterschool program. The answer to what works really depends on what the community needs. The readers are invited to take the components of the program that might work for them and use these to create or improve and evaluate their own afterschool programs—so that they will ultimately be able to create sustainable, effective, and replicable programs that can provide evidence of effectiveness. This chapter concludes with advice to invest more funding not only in afterschool program implementation but also in afterschool evaluation, for it is only when programs are able to show evidence of effectiveness that they can definitely expect to sustain themselves beyond the pilot stage.

The preparation of this book was primarily funded by a grant from the Office of Educational Research and Improvement, U.S. Department of Education (No. R117D940005), and some of the material in it began as a set of technical reports for the Center for Research on the Education of Students Placed At Risk, also funded by the U.S. Department of Education. However, any opinions expressed are those of the author alone and do not necessarily represent the positions or policies of the U.S. Department of Education or other funders.

Acknowledgments

I want to thank the many program developers, implementers, evaluators, and school personnel who have given much time and effort to providing and reviewing the information presented in this report about their programs. Their cooperation and support have been essential in maintaining accuracy of program descriptions and evaluation information. I also thank the staff members of the National Institute on Out of School Time, who took the time to provide initial comments and suggestions on drafts of this report, and thank Kim Pierce, Joan Herman, and Carla Sanger for their reviews and suggestions regarding this work. Many thanks also go to John Hollifield, Barbara Colton, Bob Slavin, and Laurence Peters, who provided positive feedback, and to Johns Hopkins University students Claire Whitner and Rebecca Zarutskie, who worked diligently. Finally, I express my deepest appreciation to Christopher Anderson, my research assistant, who was able to make this book into a reality during the final days, when completing the book became a difficult and tedious task. Thank you for the editing and for all the comments. I knew that the book was done when there were no more sticky comments to be edited. The contents of the report and interpretations of the data remain, of course, the sole responsibility of the author.

The following reviewers are also gratefully acknowledged:

Anne Dorsey
Professor, University of Cincinnati
Cincinnati, OH

Wendy Russell
Research Associate,
RMC Research Corporation
Arlington, VA

Beth Miller
Consultant, National Institute on
   Out-of-School Time
Wellesley College, Wellesley, MA

Marie Miller-Whitehead
Consultant, The Miller Group
Muscle Shoals, AL

About the Author

Olatokunbo S. Fashola is an Associate Research Scientist at the Johns Hopkins University Center for Research on the Education of Students Placed at Risk. She received her PhD in 1995 from the University of California, Santa Barbara. Her research interests include reading, afterschool programs, language development, emergent literacy, program evaluation, educational policy issues, problem solving, and bilingual education. She has written numerous articles on these various topics and is coauthor of *Show Me the Evidence! Proven and Promising Programs for America's Schools*. She has also served as principal investigator, evaluator, and advisor for several afterschool programs across the country. Her report *Review of Extended-Day and After-School Programs and Their Effectiveness* has garnered national attention. She has authored a number of articles on schoolwide reform and is coauthor of two chapters in *Effective Programs for Latino Students*. She has appeared on the television program *This Is America With Dennis Wholey* and is the recipient of an award for research excellence from the American Federation of Teachers.

Why Afterschool Programs?

The agreement is clear that students need supervision and learning opportunities during the afterschool hours, but exactly what activities to engage in and why is a large topic of debate among the very parties that agree that a need exists. Until now, the phrases *child care,* or *afterschool care,* and *school-age child care,* have intentionally not been used because these terms represent an entirely different school of thought from academically oriented afterschool programs. This is not to say that academically oriented afterschool programs are not concerned about issues such as safety, but, rather, their focus is mainly on creating afterschool programs that will enhance and improve learning opportunities for children. This book seeks to go beyond the topic of child care versus afterschool care, and address effective, academically based afterschool programs. First, though, it is important to attempt to shed some light on the topic of afterschool versus child care.

School-age child care and afterschool programs have similar concerns about children, on the one hand, and yet are very different, on the other hand; and although they can serve similar populations, they represent two different schools of thought. The similarities between the two entities lie in the students that they serve and their concerns for adequate supervision. For example, school-age child care (SACC) programs serve students in Grades K-3, and afterschool programs also serve students in this same population. A big distinction between the two entities, however, is the word *licensing.* This word lies at the heart of many of the afterschool and school-age child care debates that take place on a daily basis. To understand these debates, it is important to understand the reasons behind the various schools of thought and to remember that the children are at the heart of the debate.

It is important to make certain distinctions between the purposes of early childhood education (ECE) centers and academically based afterschool programs housed in public school buildings, with public school teachers providing the services to the children. ECE centers or sometimes day care centers, are state-licensed facilities created to provide supervised care for preschool-age children. Some centers are licensed for infants, and others have special licensing to provide child care for school-age children up to third grade (SACC centers). In addition to this, some centers, which have academic goals for their students, operate as preschool programs as opposed to only child care programs, but centers that operate as preschool programs mainly educate non-school-age children.

Most of these centers do not operate in a public school setting but, rather, in homes or in buildings other than public schools. The buildings must pass inspection by state licensing agencies that will allow them to operate in these facilities. Many of the educators have different sets of credentials they must adhere to in order to work in these centers. Once again, the main reason for the different requirements is that the students are not of school age, and the teachers are not credentialed to the same degree or nature as credentialed public school teachers are.

If early childhood education centers choose to serve older children (up to Grade 3) during the nonschool hours, they are still required to adhere to ECE standards and licensing regulations. But the license is really to run a business, which is a school-age child care business or the day care business operated by a private entity. Licensing laws for these businesses have been created by state licensing agencies, and additional standards and guidelines are created and endorsed by organizations such as the National Association for the Education of Young Children (NAEYC), the National School-Age Child Care Alliance (NSACCA), and other organizations that address these issues. These organizations address the private programs that provide child care and create standards that serve as guides that other programs providing similar services should follow.

Public schools that offer preschools also adhere to the standards as they relate to the age of the children. This means that if there is a preschool-age population being served in a public school, teachers delivering the services are expected to adhere to the state ECE licensing standards. In addition, the facilities that the children use on a daily basis must meet these standards.

The big issue of concern and sometimes contention, however, is between public schools offering afterschool programs and private programs offering afterschool care services. The philosophies behind many of these programs differ, as do the buildings in which they are held. It is sometimes perceived by the non-ECE group that the standards governing the running of the afterschool programs should differ. Those from the afterschool school of thought believe that these standards are helpful guidelines that could be useful but should not be mandatory for public schools, whereas those from the SACC school of thought believe that the standards should be mandatory for all entities providing afterschool services whether they are public or private. Many of the afterschool programs run in public schools are run by public school teachers who already have certification for teaching school-age children. In addition, many of these programs are operated in school buildings, and so whether they are required to adhere to the standards of noncertified teachers and nonpublic schools is questionable because the public afterschool programs already exceed the standards for private programs, especially if these programs are offered by public school teachers.

Now, many of the ECE standards are positive, as they speak to issues of safety and care of students. However, the relationship or the differences between day care and child care programs offered for students by private entities and by public schools must be made clear. As was previously mentioned, the standards address issues related to the staffing, environmental safety, and general safety of the students.

To SACC centers offering afterschool care during the afterschool hours, these standards must be a requirement. For public schools offering afterschool programs, the standards offer good suggestions, but one must remember that the staffing and certification of the teachers in the public schools vary from and often overrule those for private-school teachers, even during the afterschool hours.

Having said this, we also realize that many school-based afterschool programs hire and train community-based volunteers or staff members to actually lead the nonacademic classes. If students are left alone with nonpublic school certified personnel at any point, then it is best that individual personnel be required to adhere to licensing requirements. If this is a difficult goal, then the schools must be sure to have a certified teacher in the presence of the volunteer at all times. Given all the controversy surrounding afterschool programs versus child care and the various schools of thought surrounding the concerns, one still cannot dispute the fact that the safety and welfare of the children are what drive this new focus on afterschool programs. This discussion leads to the topic of why afterschool programs are offered.

The hours 3 p.m. to 6 p.m. and sometimes 3 p.m. to 10 p.m. are a time in which parents and primary caretakers of children aged 3 to 18, and sometimes from birth to age 18, are concerned about the well-being of their children. For parents of school-age children, once school is dismissed, opportunities for children's involvement in undesirable behaviors increase. However, these hours are seen by some groups, such as educators, as prime time—not only to keep children safe and out of trouble but also to provide them with help in areas of need. Some of these areas include academics, recreation, social skills, and behavior.

The creation of 21st Century Community Learning Centers (21st CCLC) and afterschool funding by foundations, legislation, school districts, and community-based organizations addresses not only a need for afterschool programs but also provides access to services for a large number of students who would otherwise not be able to afford them. The need for afterschool programs cuts across all demographic groups, and this is evident in responses to polls and surveys given by the Mott Foundation and the U.S. Department of Education (Mott Foundation, 1999). Academically based afterschool and extended-school-day programs, unlike child care programs, tend to have more of an academic focus.

In this book, academically based afterschool programs and extended-school-day programs share similar qualities and have similar goals. Those goals are usually mostly academic, with recreational, cultural, and social programs added to them. The reasons for providing academic services generally stem from the fact that many children, regardless of socioeconomic status, race, and gender tend to need additional help in academic work. Providing educational afterschool programs in a public setting provides students with credentialed teachers who can work with much smaller groups of children to improve their areas of academic weakness.

We choose to focus on academically based afterschool programs because we believe that many students need to have additional time to be involved in quality, enriching academic activities. Participation in school-based, academically oriented afterschool programs provides affordable and quality afterschool experiences for children who would not otherwise have access to such experiences. By focusing on academics, it is not the intent of this book to replicate the regular school-day experience but, rather, to provide some additional experiences that would otherwise not be available. These activities could include tutoring, academic enhancement, remediation, or other forms of academic support.

We acknowledge the existence of many different types of academically based afterschool programs, but very few have shown evidence of effectiveness, and this is what we choose to focus on initially. We are aware that some programs are in the process of collecting data on evidence of effectiveness, and we refer to evidence gathered by these programs as promising. We recognize the fact that not every single afterschool program has academic achievement at its core. For example, some community-based afterschool programs that provide services to a widespread number of students have been evaluated or have partnered with public schools. We include these programs in the community-based afterschool programs.

Finally, we include some programs that may not have been used in the afterschool programs but fulfill the needs of some (such as study skills programs) and could be adapted for use in afterschool settings. These programs have shown evidence of effectiveness during the regular school day. We expect this book to serve as a combination of theory, research, and practice for implementing effective afterschool programs for researchers, educators, practitioners, legislators, and any other groups interested in afterschool issues.

Afterschool Programs: Benefits and Challenges

Educators and policymakers have begun to show increasing interest in programs designed for use in the nonschool hours, especially those designated for afterschool (see, for example, Carnegie Corporation, 1989, 1992, 1994, 1995; Mott Foundation, 1999; Pederson, de Kanter, Bobo, Weinig, & Noeth, 1998; U.S. National Commission on Time and Learning, 1992, 1994). In recent years, a lot of emphasis has been placed on afterschool programs for three primary reasons. First, attendance in afterschool programs can provide children with supervision during a time in which many might be exposed to, and engage in, more antisocial and destructive behaviors. Second, afterschool programs can provide enriching experiences that broaden children's perspectives and improve their socialization. Third, and a more recent emphasis, afterschool programs can perhaps help improve the academic achievement of students who are not achieving as well as they need to during regular school hours.

Many children do not receive adequate supervision during the afterschool hours (Schwartz, 1996; U.S. Bureau of the Census, 1987). When the dismissal bell rings, many children go home to empty houses (latchkey children), and many others "hang out" on the streets until their parents return home. Children left unsupervised after school often fall prey to deviant behaviors that are harmful to them, to their schools, and to their communities (Bronfenbrenner, 1986; Furby & Beyth-Marom, 1990; Galambos & Maggs, 1991; Steinberg, 1986). They are more likely to be involved in delinquent acts during these hours (Bureau of Labor Statistics, 1997; Galambos & Maggs, 1991; Grossman & Garry, 1997; Schwartz, 1996). Numerous reports have documented that a high proportion of juvenile crimes are committed between 3 p.m. and 6 p.m. each day, and these reports have created increased interest in strategies that will occupy students productively during these hours (Bureau of Labor Statistics, 1997; Council of Chief State School Officers, 1987; Henderson, 1990; Jacoby, 1989; Office of Juvenile Justice and Delinquency Prevention, 1999).

For children who face academic or behavioral obstacles to success during the school hours, the afterschool hours can be a time to attempt to eliminate these barriers and improve the education of the whole child. However, accomplishing this goal is not as easy as it may seem. Concern for what happens to school-age children during the afterschool hours is not a new topic of discussion (Carnegie Council on Adolescent Development, 1994; Marx, 1989, 1990; Morris, 1992; Morton-Young, 1995; Seligson, 1986, 1988; Seligson & Allenson, 1993; U.S. Department of Education, 1993). Many studies concerning this issue have been conducted over time, asking whether supervised care is better than nonsupervised care (Galambos & Maggs, 1991), exploring differences in types of afterschool arrangements (Vandell & Corasaniti, 1988; Vandell & Ramanan, 1991) and trying to find the best types of afterschool arrangements based on the needs of the family, the child, and the resources available.

In addition to providing supervision, afterschool and extended-school-day programs are now being seen as a means of improving academic achievement, providing opportunities for academic enrichment, and providing social, cultural, and recreational activities (Boyer, 1987; Burns, 1992; Campbell & Flaker, 1985; Fashola, 1998, 1999, in press; Halpern, 1992). Recently, Congress allocated $40 million to create 21st century afterschool, community learning centers across the country, in hopes of improving the lives of children and the communities they live in during the nonschool hours, including after school and in the summer (U.S. Department of Education, 1997, 1999). In his 1998, 1999, and 2000 State of the Union addresses, President Bill Clinton substantially increased federal funding for 21st CCLC afterschool programs (Clinton, 1997, 1998, 1999, 2000). In particular, extended-day and afterschool programs have been proposed as a means of accelerating the achievement of students placed at risk of academic failure due to poverty, lack of parental support, reduced opportunities to learn, and other socioeconomic and academic factors (Frymier & Gansneder, 1989; McAdoo & Crawford, 1988; McGillis, 1996).

Although the benefits to be derived from the use of the afterschool hours seem great, the most effective ways to capitalize on this opportunity are not well understood, and existing afterschool efforts vary enormously in purposes and in operations. They range from purely day care, to purely academic, to purely enrichment programs, to various mixtures of these. Also, their costs vary greatly, as some programs can be very expensive and may take resources that could be used more appropriately for other investments.

To identify effective strategies for students outside school hours, particularly for at-risk students, it is essential to know what types of extended-day programs and particularly what specific programs are most likely to lead to valued outcomes. However, this kind of research is very limited. In some studies (Engman, 1992; Henderson, 1990; Mercure, 1993; Milch, 1986), academically based afterschool programs have been loosely linked to improving some at-risk children's academic and social skills and work habits. But this body of literature largely studies the effects of afterschool programs as a whole rather than the effects of specific effective and replicable afterschool or extended-school-day models or programs.

The evaluation of afterschool programs can be challenging (Blanton, Mayer, & Shustack, 1995). There are few studies of the effects of specific afterschool programs, and those that exist have found highly inconsistent outcomes. Selection bias is a frequent problem, as students who voluntarily attend various afterschool programs may be different from those who do not choose to do so. Furthermore, the limited research has primarily involved middle-income, Caucasian students, making the results difficult to generalize to disadvantaged or minority children. Circumstances surrounding the type of care provided, the kinds of students who attended the different programs, and what the programs themselves entailed have rarely been studied in detail. Different studies have yielded different answers to different questions about different issues relating to afterschool child care.

In addition, afterschool programs and the regular school-day programs are not directly connected, so studying the effects of the afterschool program on regular school-day academics is difficult. Afterschool programs may exist in community centers, in clubs, or on school grounds, and they may serve students from many different schools.

Afterschool Programs and Their Functions

Before addressing the effects of programs that take place in the afterschool hours, it is important to define the various types of programs and their purposes. In this book, we distinguish between three different types of afterschool arrangements: day care, afterschool, and extended-school-day programs. Each of these types of programs addresses different issues and has different strengths.

Day Care Programs

Day care programs do not necessarily have an academic focus or goals (although some may); instead, they emphasize recreational and cultural activities. They are seldom aligned with academic instruction provided during the regular school day, although many do provide homework assistance. Although some day care programs may also have small academic components, the main goal of day care programs is to provide students whose parents are working or otherwise engaged with a safe haven. The period of operation for typical, afterschool, day care programs is between 3 p.m. and 6 p.m., and the programs typically emphasize safety, a positive climate, and enjoyable cultural and recreational activities. Such programs primarily involve children from preschool to third grade. Licensing is required for day care program staff, and many also require child development associate degrees. A main distinguishing factor is that day care programs require licensing for the sites and the workers, whereas school-based afterschool programs do not necessarily require licensing, as they serve school-age children.

Afterschool Programs

Afterschool programs are more likely to involve school-age children only (ages 5 to 18) and emphasize academic as well as nonacademic activities. Compared to day care programs, afterschool programs are more likely to provide transportation, a wider variety of recreational programs, and increased child-to-adult ratios. These programs are usually more affordable than day care programs. Examples of afterschool programs include Boys & Girls Clubs, the YMCA, Big Brothers/Big Sisters, some 4-H programs, ASPIRA (which in Spanish means aspiration), church programs, and municipal parks and recreation programs.

Some afterschool programs offer specialized activities, using professionals or qualified persons and volunteers to provide instruction in such areas as ballet, tap dancing, music, karate, and chess. These programs seek to help children make creative use of their free time. Students may enroll in these classes, or parents may enroll them, purely out of interest in the skills, not to satisfy any child care needs. The classes often provide progress information to the children and to the instructors through, for example, badges or promotions to higher ranks in the Boy Scouts and Girl Scouts, recitals in musical classes, and tournaments in karate or chess classes. The classes provide children with opportunities to explore and develop skills, talents, and hobbies and, later, to show these skills to their parents and others. Academic achievement, attendance, or other school-related outcomes may or may not be primary or secondary goals of these programs.

School-Based, Academic, Extended-Day Programs

This type of program takes place during the same afterschool hours but differs from day care and afterschool programs in that it is directly connected to what takes place during the school day. Although day care and afterschool programs may or may not take place on the school grounds, the school-based, academic, extended-day program typically takes place inside the school building and provides a mixture of academic, recreational, and cultural programs. Regular school-day teachers and paraprofessionals are usually paid to stay at the school during the afterschool hours.

As noted in its name, this type of model has a main academic focus, and the goals, outcomes, and methods of academic instruction are directly related to and aligned with what happens during the day. Teachers conduct small-group or tutorial remedial classes, supervise homework clubs, and teach study skills and advanced or supplementary courses (e.g., a foreign language or an advanced science). In addition, paraprofessionals and community volunteers may provide cultural and recreational programs. Teachers may also supervise and train volunteers or paraprofessionals to provide academic or nonacademic services. Extended-school-day programs can be schoolwide or districtwide. They are rarely mandatory but may provide greater or lesser inducements for children to attend.

Some programs invite community members to their program planning sessions and include them as teachers for some of the classes and activities. These individuals may be associated with churches (e.g., Child First Authority), private and public corporations (e.g., Help One Student To Succeed), law enforcement agencies (e.g., Police Athletic League), parent groups (e.g., PTAs), businesses, members of the armed forces (e.g., On a Roll), and other groups. In some cases, they make the afterschool program a hub of community activity, and over time, the program and the school may begin to have a broad impact on the community.

One recent trend in some extended-day programs is the development of curricula tied to district, state, and national goals yet designed to be taught afterschool. Such programs may involve well-designed curricula, teacher training, and student assessments. These programs provide students with complete, well-tested approaches, resources, trainers, and so on, reducing the need for every school to reinvent the wheel. Some such programs seem promising, have been widely used, and have at least anecdotal indications of effectiveness in individual schools that have made gains. However, many have not been used with at-risk students and, although they may have been assessed for implementation and enjoyment, few have been evaluated for achievement purposes using methods that would pass even the most minimal standards.

Focus and Methodology of the Review

The goal of this book is to examine current afterschool and extended-school-day programs, both to review the limited research on the effects of these programs on student achievement and to describe promising strategies that communities can use in partnership with schools to create effective afterschool programs for all children in elementary and secondary schools. It is implicit that all the programs mentioned have been used with at-risk students.

This book identifies and describes programs with an educational focus that have been shown to have evidence of effectiveness for all children during the nonschool hours. We also include some programs that have little evidence of effectiveness as yet but do have active dissemination and replicability materials that could be used by other afterschool programs. Not all the programs in this book were developed specifically for use after school. Some have been adapted for use during the afterschool hours, and others are adaptable. For programs that can be adapted for use during the nonschool hours, the evidence of effectiveness presented is usually not from use after school but from use as supplementary programs during the regular school day.

This book summarizes but does not examine in detail the benefits of different types of day care, which are presented in various other studies (see, for example, studies like Galambos & Maggs, 1991; Posner & Vandell, 1994; Seligson, 1988, 1986; Seligson & Allenson, 1993; Steinberg, 1986; Vandell & Corasaniti, 1988; Vandell & Ramanan, 1991). Ideally, this book would identify only programs that have strong evidence of effectiveness and of replicability based on use in afterschool academic settings, and these are the criteria used in our identification and description of the programs. As has been mentioned earlier, however, as this is a relatively new field of research, not many programs fully meet our criteria.

Effectiveness

Programs were considered to be effective if evaluations compared students who participated in the program to similar students, in matched comparison or control schools, and found the program students to perform significantly better on fair measures of academic performance. Such evaluations were required to demonstrate that experimental and control students were initially equivalent on measures of academic performance and socioeconomic status and on other measures and were similar in other ways. *Fair measures* were ones assessing the objectives pursued equally by experimental and control groups; for example, a curriculum-specific measure would be fair only if the control group implemented the same curriculum.

Many studies of innovative programs and evaluations compared gains made by program students on standardized tests, usually expressed in percentiles or normal curve equivalents (NCEs), to expected gains derived from national norming samples. This design, widely used in evaluation of Chapter 1/Title 1 programs, is prone to error and generally overstates program impacts (see Slavin & Madden, 1991). Programs evaluated using NCE gains or other alternatives to experimental-control comparisons are discussed as promising if their outcomes are particularly striking, but such data are not considered conclusive. We exclude after-the-fact comparisons of experimental and control groups after outcomes are known.

Replicability

The best evidence that a program is replicable in other sites is that it has been, in fact, replicated elsewhere, especially if there is evidence that the program was evaluated and found to be effective in sites beyond its initial pilot locations. The existence of an active dissemination effort is also a strong indication of replicability. Programs are considered low in replicability if they have been used in a small number of schools and appear to depend on conditions (e.g., charismatic principals, magnet schools, extraordinary resources) unlikely to exist on a significant scale elsewhere.

Literature Search Procedures

The broadest possible search was carried out for programs that had been evaluated and that applied to students in afterschool settings. Some of the sources of information for this review were the National Diffusion Network (NDN), Educational Resources Information Centers (ERIC), education journals, conferences attended, and personal communications. The NDN was a part of the U.S. Department of Education until the network's end in 1996. A Joint Dissemination Review Panel (JDRP), later called the Program Effectiveness Panel (PEP), identified promising programs that had evidence of evaluation and possible effectiveness, and these programs then qualified for dissemination through the NDN. Evaluation requirements for these programs were not rigorous, however, and many of the evaluations looked only at pre-post and NCE gains as evidence of effectiveness.

Effect Sizes

Evidence of effectiveness in this review is reported in the form of effect sizes or NCEs. An *effect size* is the proportion of a standard deviation by which an experimental group exceeds a control group. To give a sense of scale, an effect size of + 1.0 would be equivalent to 100 points on the Stanford Achievement Test scale, 2 stanines, 15 IQ points, or about 21 NCEs (Fashola & Slavin, 1998b). In general, an effect size of + 0.25 or more would be considered educationally significant.

Types of Programs and Their Evaluations

Thirty-four programs met the inclusion criteria stated in this book. Programs included fell into one of four major categories. The first category includes programs that address a specific academic component of the curriculum—language arts. Programs in this category are regularly used as supplements to the regular school-day program but have been used during the nonschool hours. The second category consists of afterschool programs that address other specific areas of the curriculum, such as science or computer technology. This category also includes specific for-profit programs developed as enrichment programs specifically for use after school. The third category includes tutoring programs aimed at improving reading. These differ from the programs in the first category primarily because many of these programs are one-on-one tutoring programs. Some are adaptable for use in afterschool settings, and some are not. This category also includes study skills programs. These programs influence all areas of the curriculum but focus mainly on teaching study and comprehension skills to low achievers. The fourth category consists of community-based afterschool programs. These programs are not necessarily academic in nature but are sometimes located in schools and sometimes operated as community-based and community-owned programs. In addition to these four types, we include programs that could serve as add-on cultural and recreational components of afterschool or extended-school-day programs, as this is an important part of afterschool developments and activities.

The following chapters describe some of the most widely used afterschool and extended-day programs. We present the current state of the evidence, if any, and the apparent replicability of the model, especially with students placed at risk. In searching for evaluations and evidence of effectiveness, we emphasized studies that used experimental and control groups that were evaluated on appropriate measures of achievement and other outcomes. The study included well-matched treatment and comparison groups that were also evaluated using the same measures. All the programs described in this book are used in schools, except for some of the community-based programs.

2

Language Arts Afterschool Programs

The first group of programs in this book consists of programs designed to provide assistance to students experiencing difficulties or programs designed to provide enriching opportunities for students in language arts. They have all been evaluated for use among all students, including students at risk. However, only one program in this section was specifically designed as an afterschool program for students at risk and has been evaluated for that population (Extended-Day Tutoring Program in Memphis). The remaining programs in this section are presented as possible programs that can be used in afterschool settings.

Books and Beyond

Books and Beyond (Books and Beyond, 1995; Topolovac, 1982a, 1982b) is a voluntary reading program aimed at helping and motivating students in Grades K-8 to read more recreationally and watch less television. The program strives to help students become more critical about the types of television shows that they watch. With the combination of discriminating television watching and enjoyable recreational reading, the ultimate goal of Books and Beyond is to improve reading skills and to improve students' attitudes toward books and reading. Students earn small awards, such as theme folders, pencils, and gold medals if they read a certain number of books, depending on grade level. Books and Beyond supplements the school's regular reading program and has also been implemented in afterschool or extended-school-day programs.

When schools implement Books and Beyond, they develop a coordinating team that consists of the principal, library-media specialist, three teachers, and three parents. All teachers are informed about the program and encouraged to participate by reading aloud to their classes on a regular basis and by acting as role models who record their own recreational reading. The main implementation and operation of the program are usually the responsibility of the core team—including parents—rather than of the individual classroom teacher.

When afterschool programs implement the afterschool version of Books and Beyond, the core team consists of a director and two or three staff coordina-

13

tors who take on the responsibilities of the core team. In addition, older students (junior high school and high school students) can be used as reading models, and they, along with parents, are responsible for keeping track of the books read.

The intended audience for this program is all students from varying socioeconomic-status (SES) backgrounds, including gifted, at-risk, special education, and bilingual students. Nonreaders can participate in the program by having books read to them; readers can include tutors, study buddies, community readers, and caregivers. Schools operate Books and Beyond for 6 to 8 months, allowing sufficient time to build positive reading habits, and the program is implemented in the form of a read-a-thon.

Books and Beyond includes a parental component. Parent volunteers coordinate the record-keeping activities of the program, including tracking the books read by the students and the various awards presented. The program asks parents who work with the program at home to read to their children, take them to the public library, help them keep records of the books they read at home and at school, chart the amount of time they spend watching television, and model reading themselves.

Students in kindergarten through third grade have a goal of 120 books over the course of the program that they are required to read or have read to them if they wish to earn a gold medal award at the end of the program. Children in Grades 4-8 are required to read 2,400 pages to obtain a gold medal. These goals are adaptable, depending on the needs of the children involved in the program. Books and Beyond typically receives support and endorsement from local businesses. Read-a-thon theme topics include Travel Through Time, Jog America, Quest for Knowledge, Sports Decathlon, Around the World With Books, and Mysteries of the Deep.

The evaluations of Books and Beyond do not include evaluations of the program in afterschool or extended-school-day settings. The pilot evaluation of Books and Beyond was done in three evaluation sites (Books and Beyond, 1983), and the replication evaluation included a diverse group of students. In a Missouri study, the students in Grades 2-8 were predominantly Caucasian, middle-class students. In a Connecticut study, the students were in Grades 2-6 and were of a variety of ethnic backgrounds. These students had been labeled at risk for dropping out of school. Finally, students in a New York study were in Grades 2-8, were of a variety of ethnic backgrounds, and had shown very low standardized-test scores. The evaluation consisted of surveys of the students and their parents about the number of hours that the students had spent watching television as well as the number of books the students had read during the program. Students involved in the evaluations did not include all the participants in the program but, rather, students who had read a minimum number of books (for example, 60 books in Grades 2-3). Surveys were administered at the beginning and end of the sessions. The original study included a control group, but the differences in responses between the treatment and control groups were not statistically significant. All students, experimental as well as control, stated that they had decreased the amount of time they spent watching television, increased discrimination in their selection of television programs, increased the number of books they read, would be more likely to choose to read a book than watch television (compared to the beginning of the program), and read more at home.

The limitations of these studies are clear. They rely on self-report data only and have no assessment of actual gains in reading achievement. The gains that were noted on pre-to-post surveys were also seen among nonparticipants, and the studies were limited to students who had read at least a certain number of books. These findings can be considered only suggestive at best.

Books and Beyond currently exists in over 5,000 schools in 45 states, has been expanded to the preschool level with the Ready to Read program, and has also been adopted by 130 elementary schools in the United Kingdom. Books and Beyond has also been used as a stand-alone, afterschool and extended-school-day program in schools, in boys' and girls' clubs, and in some afterschool community efforts in low-income housing projects. Books and Beyond has added a new program titled Math, Science, and Beyond, which seeks to teach children mathematics and science during the afterschool hours. This program is currently being developed and evaluated under the auspices of a National Science Foundation grant for use in afterschool programs.

Junior Great Books Curriculum of Interpretive Reading, Writing, and Discussion (JGBC)

The Junior Great Books Curriculum of Interpretive Reading, Writing, and Discussion is a junior version of the Great Books Foundation program (Criscuola, 1994; Friertag & Chernoff, 1987; Kuenzer, 1978; Nichols, 1992, 1993; Will, 1986). It strives to promote cognitive processing in reading comprehension and literacy in children in Grades 2-12 by emphasizing three kinds of thinking: factual, interpretive, and evaluative. These three types of information about text are explored by children using a method of shared inquiry and interpretive questioning, which encourages children to realize that there is more than one answer to questions asked about the text they have read.

The JGBC is not a stand-alone program but is used as a partial replacement of, or supplement to, the regular reading program during the regular school day. Some activities that the children in the JGBC program participate in include text-opener, reading the story twice, sharing questions, directed notes, interpreting words, shared inquiry discussion, and writing after the discussion.

When a school chooses to engage in the JGBC program, it is provided with a 2-day, 10-hour, Basic Leader training course. Schools can also choose to enroll in optional 1- or 2-day curriculum leader training courses. During this training, core leaders are taught to conduct activities such as preparing units and discussing interpretive issues together. Students who participate in the program are usually enrolled for one semester, in which they study an anthology consisting of 12 selections.

In an evaluation of JGBC that researched the effects of the program on academic achievement in reading vocabulary during the school day, 150 JGBC students were matched with 120 control students in four schools, and tested on the Iowa Test of Basic Skills (ITBS)—three schools—and California Test of Basic Skills (CTBS)—one school. This study included both urban and suburban populations. The JGBC schools on each site involved a control classroom and a treatment (JGBC) classroom. Teachers were randomly assigned to a group (using a coin flip) to determine whether they would be in the control group or the experimental group. In four of the schools, JGBC students outscored their control group counterparts (ES = + .24, + .34, + .39, and + .32). An additional internal evaluation of the program showed that students involved in JGBC demonstrated stronger interpretive thinking skills than did the students in the control group.

These results show the effects of JGBC in programs used during the school day and not after school. JGBC was not originally created for use in afterschool settings and has not been evaluated for such use but has often been used in that way. The creators of the program are able and willing to help afterschool programs implement JGBC in their specific programs either with teachers or paraprofessionals (volunteers, parents, and college students). JGBC exists in schools across the country.

Extended-Day Tutoring Program in Memphis City Schools

In 1995, the Center for Research in Educational Policy at the University of Memphis developed an extended-day tutoring program for use in the public schools (Ross, Smith, Casey, & Slavin, 1996). This program was piloted in Memphis, Tennessee, for the first year. The goal of the program was to improve reading performances of students in Grades 2-4 by group tutoring the children during the afterschool hours using a language arts curriculum. The program was mainly academic, using materials adapted from the Success for All (SFA) reading program (Slavin, Madden, Dolan, & Wasik, 1996) and other reading strategies.

Teachers were trained in how to tutor students in reading using the Story Telling and Retelling (STaR) method used in SFA, as well as others, and used the Scott Foresman reading series. Some but not all of the schools involved in the program were Success for All schools during the regular day. Students were selected for the program based on their need for additional instruction. They were taught how to read and retell the stories assigned to them, using

STaR, and to use additional follow-up activities and strategies, such as partner reading. Students enrolled in the program attended the extended-day tutoring program between 1 and 4 hours each week. After their language arts lessons, they had opportunities to engage in cultural, recreational, and other academic enrichment programs, such as book clubs, computer skill-building activities, and test-taking strategies.

The participants in the study included 656 Title 1 students in Grades 2-4. Half of the students participated in the program, and half of them did not. The students were randomly selected for each group, but they were matched on the basis of standardized-test scores, attitude, behavior, grade, and age. When the students were compared at the beginning of the project, students did not differ in their test scores. The evaluation consisted of two parts: formative and summative. The formative part of the evaluation consisted of a teacher survey and observation forms that measured level of implementation of the tutoring program. The summative part of the evaluation measured Tennessee Comprehensive Assessment Program (TCAP) scores at the end of the session.

Two issues that plague evaluations of nonmandatory afterschool programs are attendance and selection of a control group. Both were factors in this study. The average attendance for the afterschool tutoring program was 75%. For the study, the treatment group consisted of students who attended the program at least 50% of the time for some of the analyses, and for others, at least 80%. The students who did not attend, or who had low attendance, were added to the control group. The two groups were compared in various ways, using prereading-test scores as the covariates. Overall, the greater the attendance rates, the more likely the students were to perform slightly better than their counterparts, with effect sizes ranging from +.11 to +.23. In addition, students in third grade who attended 80% of the time or more were more likely to do significantly better than their counterparts in the control group and also better than their counterparts in Grades 2 and 4 of the treatment and control groups. The total increase in the number of NCE points for students in third grade was 8.5, and it was lower for students in other grades.

Difficulties in finding an appropriate control group also affected this study. For example, 11 of the 13 schools showed correlations of +.94 or higher on the pretests between the control and treatment group students, but one school showed a moderate correlation (+.47), and another school showed a negative correlation (−.10), suggesting that the control groups and the experimental groups were not well matched. The initial analyses described above included the outlier groups.

Murfreesboro Extended School Program (ESP)

One of the most widely known, community-based, extended-day school programs is the Murfreesboro Extended School Program (ESP) in Murfreesboro, Tennessee. This program began in 1986 at one elementary school (Jones, 1994, 1995). The program has a clear academic focus but also includes cultural and recreational elements.

The hours of the Extended School Program are from 6 a.m. until 7:45 a.m. and then after school from 2:25 p.m. until 6 p.m. At the end of the school day, students involved in the ESP program are divided into groups of 12 and provided with a qualified staff person who provides academic enrichment and support. Each day for 30 minutes, students are provided with tutors from Middle Tennessee State University, parents, and staff members from the school, who help them with their homework. Following this, the students involved in the program are able to choose additional academic skills classes in which they learn basic reading skills and basic mathematics skills, geography, science, study skills, and other higher-order thinking skills, using the Paideia philosophy as the basis for the curriculum and instructional program. The Paideia program, based on the work of Mortimer Adler (1982), emphasizes engaging all students in intellectual inquiry, with a particular focus on great books and great thinkers. It uses small group "Socratic" seminars, coaching by teachers, peer tutoring, project-based learning, and other means of engaging students as active learners. Paideia principles are used as a general guide to reform, not as a specific strategy.

Cultural activities include music, violin and guitar, arts, computer clubs, and foreign language. In addition, students have opportunities to engage in recreational activities, such as physical education, movies, handicrafts, dance, Brownies, and 4-H.

The Extended School Program is now institutionalized in the Murfreesboro School district, with support from the central school district as well as site-based support. About 2,000 of the 5,700 students were involved in the 2000-2001 school year. Each school has a staff person provided by the district, the equivalent of a half-time assistant principal, who is mainly responsible for the extended school program.

The ESP program does not have evidence of effectiveness. It exists only in Murfreesboro but has been sustained for 11 years.

Coca-Cola Valued Youth Program (VYP)

The Coca-Cola Valued Youth Program (1991) is a cross-age tutoring program designed to increase the self-esteem and school success of at-risk middle and high school students by placing them in positions of responsibility as tutors of younger, elementary school students. The Intercultural Development Research Association in San Antonio, Texas, originally developed the Valued Youth Program. The original implementation of the program was funded by Coca-Cola and implemented in collaboration with five school districts in San Antonio between 1984 and 1988, with approximately 525 high school tutors and 1,575 elementary tutees involved.

The overall goal of the program is to reduce the dropout rates of at-risk students by improving their self-concepts and academic skills. Making them tutors and providing assistance with basic academic skills does this. The program also emphasizes elimination of nonacademic and disciplinary factors that contribute to dropping out. For example, it attempts to develop students' senses of self-control, decrease student truancy, and reduce disciplinary referrals. It also seeks to form home-school partnerships to increase the level of support available to students.

When students agree to serve as tutors, they are required to enroll in a special tutoring class, which allows them to improve their own basic academic skills as well as their tutoring skills. The students who are involved as tutors are paid a minimum-wage stipend. The tutors work with three elementary students at a time for a total of about 4 hours per week. They are taught to develop self-awareness and pride, which is expected to make them less likely to exhibit disciplinary problems. Functions are held to honor and recognize the tutors as role models. They receive T-shirts, caps, and certificates of merit for their efforts.

The main evaluation of the Coca-Cola Valued Youth Program compared 63 VYP tutors to 70 students in a comparison group (Cardenas, Montecel, Supik, & Harris, 1992). The students in four San Antonio schools were matched on the basis of age, ethnicity, lunch eligibility, percentage of students retained in grade, scores on reading tests, quality of school life, and self-concept. They were selected (not randomly) for the experimental group based on scheduling and availability, and the remaining students were placed into the comparison group. Nearly all the students in both groups were Latino and limited in English proficiency. The control students were somewhat less likely to qualify for free lunch or to have been retained in grade.

Two years after the program began, 12% of the comparison students but only 1% of the VYP students had dropped out. Reading grades were significantly higher for the VYP group as were scores on a self-esteem measure and on a measure of attitude toward school.

The VYP has been widely replicated throughout the Southwest and elsewhere. In 1990, Coca-Cola provided additional funding for sites in California, Florida, New York, and Texas, and the program is now being extended into schools in Idaho, Oregon, Montana, and other states. The Coca-Cola VYP has also been used in afterschool settings.

Project Success Enrichment (PSE)

Project Success Enrichment (PSE, 1995) was originally developed to enrich the language arts of gifted and talented students (including low-income students) in elementary schools during the regular school day by providing them with learning activities that include higher-order thinking skills, cooperative learning, interactive discussions, and shared decision making. Since its original development, it has been used among children of varying socio-economic, racial, and academic achievement levels. Teachers who incorporate PSE into their curriculum attend a 2-day workshop and learn how to adapt their curriculum to the program's goals. Teachers plan their PSE curriculum in a structured and hierarchical manner specified by the model. Project Success Enrichment uses a whole-language approach to teach language arts, incorporating reading, writing, and thinking and connecting them to specific academic processes. Students work on such language arts skills as imagery (use of metaphors and similes), vocabulary, sentences, literature, and formatting their work. They engage in writing short stories and poetry, drafting and editing their work, analyzing literature, and completing and evaluating projects.

Although PSE has a language arts and a visual arts K-12 component, the area that received validation from the National Diffusion Network (NDN) was language arts in Grades 4-6 when used during the regular school day. In the main evaluation of PSE, the language arts performance of over 700 PSE students in gifted programs in Grades 3-7 was compared to a control group, using an alternative assessment developed and validated by Sebesta (PSE, 1995). The work of all the students in both the control and the experimental groups was randomly paired (using a random number table) and then given to the evaluators. Evaluators were asked to evaluate the products with ratings of whether the portfolio products were better than those of an average gifted student for the grade level being assessed, without knowing which students belonged to which groups. Results were analyzed using the sign test (for readers knowledgeable about statistics—effect sizes were calculated using Cohen's g). Overall, gifted students who had received PSE outperformed comparison gifted students with respect to the number of "better" ratings. All the differences between the two groups showed effect sizes between +.44 and +.50.

PSE is also involved in other national and developmental projects such as Applying Technology in Rural Education (ATIRE) and Project Step-Up.

Exemplary Center for Reading Instruction (ECRI)

The goal of ECRI (Reid, 1989) is to improve elementary school students' reading ability. This program emphasizes such reading-related skills as word recognition, study skills, spelling, penmanship, proofing, and writing skills, leading to improvement in decoding, comprehension, and vocabulary. ECRI has been developed and evaluated as a regular school-day and afterschool program.

ECRI teachers expect all students to excel. The lessons for ECRI are scripted and incorporate multisensory and sequential methods and strategies of teaching. In a typical lesson, teachers introduce new concepts in lessons using at least seven methods of instruction, teaching at least one comprehension skill, one study skill, and one grammar or creative writing skill. Initially, teachers prompt students for answers. As the students begin to master the information presented, fewer and fewer prompts are provided until students can perform independently.

In one evaluation of ECRI (Reid, 1989) during the regular school day, researchers investigated the effects of ECRI on students in Grades 2-7 in Morgan County, Tennessee, and compared them to students in a control group who were using a commercial reading program. Both schools were tested using the Stanford Achievement Test reading and comprehension vocabulary subtests. ECRI students outperformed those in the control group, with effect sizes ranging from +.48 to +.90 in reading comprehension and from +.31 to +1.40 in vocabulary. Another evaluation of the effectiveness of ECRI on Latino bilingual students in Oceanside, California; Killeen, Texas; and Calexico, California (Reid, 1989), showed NCE gains that ranged from +6.4 to +25.7.

Although ECRI has been used mostly as a language arts program, it has also been frequently used as an afterschool, remedial tutoring program. The ECRI afterschool program began as a remedial tutoring program at Brigham Young University in Utah, with goals of improving the reading skills of special education students and high school students who were behind in reading. The program currently exists as a reading clinic, in which future and current teachers are trained to help students with reading difficulties, using the ECRI method.

The main evaluation of ECRI as an afterschool program used volunteers to tutor two groups of randomly assigned students who were experiencing reading difficulties (Muir, 1974). The experimental group was taught using a generic reading intervention. ECRI students received lessons in reading, writing, and spelling. At the end of the school year, students in both groups were tested using a standardized test (Durrell Analysis of Reading Difficulty), which showed that ECRI students had made significantly greater gains (ES = +1.21). The ECRI tutored group also outscored control students on each of the Durrell test scores.

Summary

Table 2.1 presents a brief overview of categories of the language arts afterschool programs presented. Although all of these programs have an afterschool focus and have been widely replicated, only three of the seven programs reviewed in this chapter (Memphis extended-day tutoring program, Murfreesboro ESP, and ECRI) were designed specifically for afterschool purposes. As was mentioned earlier, the fact that a program shows evidence of effectiveness does not necessarily mean that it *qualifies* as having evidence of effectiveness. In this case, only two of the programs mentioned in this chapter (Memphis extended-day tutoring program and ECRI) provide evidence of effectiveness in afterschool settings. This does not imply that the programs without showing evidence of effectiveness after school will not yield the desired results. They have been included in the chapter because they show evidence of promise during the afterschool hours, based on their evidence of effectiveness during the regular school day. These programs should be evaluated in afterschool settings to see whether they can, indeed, provide evidence of effectiveness during the afterschool hours and in afterschool settings. Afterschool programs intending to use these programs should engage in evaluations so that they will also provide evidence of effectiveness during the afterschool hours.

Table 2.1   Categorization of Language Arts Afterschool Programs

Program Name	Grades Served	Afterschool Focus	Widely Replicated	Specially Designed for After School	Evaluated in Afterschool Settings	Evidence of Effectiveness After School	Academically Oriented
Books and Beyond	K-8	Yes	Yes	No	No	No	Yes
Junior Great Books Curriculum	2-12	Yes	Yes	No	No	No	Yes
Extended-Day Tutoring Program (Memphis)	2-4	Yes	Yes	Yes	Yes	Yes	Yes
Mufreesboro Extended School Program	K-6	Yes	No/Partially	Yes	No	No	Yes
Coca-Cola Valued Youth Program	K-12	Yes	Yes	No	No	No	Yes
Project Success Enrichment	K-12	Yes	Yes	No	No	No	Yes
Exemplary Center for Reading Instruction	1-12	Yes	Yes	Partially	Yes	Yes	Yes

3

Enrichment Afterschool Programs

T his chapter consists of independent (sometimes commercial) programs developed specifically for use in afterschool settings. Five of the programs (Voyager, HOSO, Explore, Mindsurf, and Foundations) were developed and are used by private organizations. These programs are currently being implemented in afterschool settings across the country.

Voyager Expanded Learning

Voyager Expanded Learning is an extended-school-day (before and after school, summer, and intersession) program. It has a variety of academically enriching themes designed to help elementary school children in Grades K-6 become active learners in mathematics, reading, science, arts, and social studies.

When a school adopts the Voyager model, a district administrator is selected to conduct training sessions prior to the implementation of the program and to serve as a facilitator whenever problems may arise. Reporting to the district director is a site director, typically a teacher in the participating school. This person receives weekly training in the philosophy, curriculum, and teaching methods and then facilitates execution of the program with a maximum of 18 children per class.

Using a curriculum designed by a staff of curriculum writers in collaboration with subject area experts, the Voyager Expanded Learning program has designed curriculum units in reading (Timewarp), math (Lightspeed), biology (Dragonfly), business (Success City), the arts (Kaleidoscope), history (Marco Polo), astronomy (Spaceship of the Imagination), physics (Mainspring), archaeology and anthropology (Ice Age), and health (Pre+Med), among others. The goal of these units is to make learning interactive and meaningful by providing a cognitively stimulating yet hands-on approach to learning and problem solving in the various areas. The units are divided into daily activities, with active learning projects and outcome objectives for the teachers and the students. The development of the curriculum is research based, and the lessons for each theme are aligned with state and national standards.

Until now, results reported are based largely on teacher-parent surveys, supported by an independent study conducted by the Houston Independent School District involving over 950 students in the control group. The major evaluation has not reported results as yet. On average, results of the analysis showed that students in both groups made gains in math and reading. The results of the information obtained in this study are limited in their generalizability, as it is unknown how the students were selected to be in the two groups. The issue of selection bias was not addressed in the study. Results of the Houston Independent School District study showed that students enjoyed the program, and teachers and administrators felt that it helped the students and that they would use it again. Voyager currently has sites in over 250 schools across the country and is expanding rapidly. The program is currently undergoing an extensive evaluation process using nationally recognized experts.

Hands On Science Outreach (HOSO)

Hands On Science Outreach is an extended-school-day and afterschool program developed to encourage all children, including minority, low-income, and at-risk students, in Grades pre-K to 6 to have fun learning science and to learn by example and experience that anyone can engage in scientific inquiry. HOSO aims to improve problem-solving skills and confidence in participating in science activities.

When schools and community groups adopt HOSO, they are provided with adult leader, training activities, program activities, and materials that children are able to take home. These include everyday materials such as paper, water, rubber bands, tapes, and other common things that children can use to perform scientific experiments both during the afterschool hours and at home. The activities are divided into grade levels pre-K, K-1, 2-3, and 4-6 and are carried out in 8-week sessions each year.

Hands On Science Outreach was evaluated in 1993 by Sierra Research Associates (Goodman & Rylander, 1993) to investigate the effects of the program on children's attitudes and understanding of hands-on science during one session (8 weeks). The study consisted of 51 HOSO participants and 39 control group students. Control students attended the same schools and were in the same classes and grades as the participants. Students were not randomly selected to participate in the program, but they were matched with the control groups on the basis of grade. The assessment tool used in the study included interviews and questions about scientific inquiry, student recollections of what they had been taught during the 8-week class, and student perceptions of who can do science and what it takes to do science.

Results of the analysis showed that the HOSO participants made statistically significant gains in their understandings compared to the control group. At the end of the evaluation, the HOSO students understood what science involved and displayed significantly better content knowledge and significantly better understanding and perceptions of who can do science, as compared to the control group. Other results showed that within the HOSO group, children who were able to recall the information about what had happened during the previous 8 weeks did better when asked, "What is science?" than students who did not recall as much.

Parents of the students were surveyed to see if their children showed any interest in science at home. Anecdotally, parents of children who scored higher grades on the assessment reported that their children showed more interest in science. Results also showed an instructor effect; the more highly the teachers were rated by the observers, the better the students recalled the information.

This study exhibits many of the characteristics endemic to many afterschool evaluation studies. As students were self-selected, they can be assumed to have higher motivation. The assessment focused on the specific material taught in the program, to which the control students were not exposed. The evaluation results, therefore, can be seen only as suggestive, not as conclusive or as evidence of effectiveness. Hands On Science Outreach currently exists in 26 states and the District of Columbia and in 250 schools and sites around the country.

Fifth Dimension

Fifth Dimension is a cognitively based, extended-school-day program, developed at the Laboratory of Comparative Human Cognition (LCHC) of the University of California at San Diego (Blanton et al., 1995; Blanton, Moorman, Hayes, & Warner, 1996; Cole, 1994a, 1994b; Laboratory of Comparative Human Cognition, 1994).

The program operates from a Vygotskyan perspective, based on the theory that exposing young children to increased opportunities to learn academic and social skills in collaboration with more capable others enables them to develop their academic and social skills. The program stresses social interaction, communication, and problem solving in approaching the various tasks. The children are given choices about what tasks to learn but are required to follow directions.

Each of the sites creates a mythical creature that also serves as a mentor to the students. Each mythical creature is created with input from the students, and its role is to serve as a sounding board, mentor, and friend to the children. All the creatures live inside the computer and enjoy receiving e-mail messages from the students. Students in the program update the creature about their progress, celebrate their successes, share their frustrations, and seek advice from the creature as they work on their tasks. In addition, the students have their peers and college students or other volunteers serve as mentors when solving their tasks.

Each program has a site coordinator, who serves as a bridge between the entity in which the program exists (e.g., Boys & Girls Clubs, YMCA, church) and the sponsoring, training entity (e.g., the university). The program coordinator is responsible for the day-to-day running of the program and for troubleshooting. The staff of the program mainly consists of undergraduates from local universities (preferably, from the sponsoring institute). Prior to working in the program, the undergraduates enroll in a cognition class that explores theories of learning, language, culture, literacy, and cognition. They become *junior researchers*, take field notes, observe interactions between children, and attempt to interpret their observations. Then, the undergraduates enter into the Fifth Dimension program, in which they serve as assistants to and mentors for the students as they guide them through the maze.

Fifth Dimension emphasizes active learning through playing. In this program, most of the activities use computers, with the exception of a few manual board games. In the afterschool programs, the Fifth Dimension is a maze or a map of tasks that each student must navigate to finally become a *wizard's assistant*. Each step on the map is usually characterized as a room, and each room has three tasks. Each of these tasks has three levels (beginning, middle, and expert). The types of tasks are developed to meet the needs of the students, and each maze is personalized. Before the students move from one activity to the next, they must complete the requirements of the activity at all three levels. After completing one activity, the students have the opportunity to either move to the next linear task or to go to the *dare room*, in which they can choose any activity they like. As the students progress through the maze, they earn points, certificates, and merit badges. When the participants have completed the tasks, they receive certificates and awards that recognize them as wizards' assistants.

The program is intended to enhance work-study habits, social skills, social consciousness, working with peers, following instructions, and problem solving, and to improve academic achievement in mathematics, reading, and word problems.

Numerous site-based evaluations have investigated the effects of participation in the program on various cognitive and academic outcomes. However, because participation in this program is voluntary it was difficult to find an appropriate control group. The program established experimental groups by selecting students who had attended at least a minimum number of sessions. Control groups generally consisted of students who did not attend the program at all. As a result of the voluntary nature of the program, at some of the sites, turnover made it difficult to establish an experimental group.

Effects of participation in Fifth Dimension were assessed on near transfer, medium transfer, and far transfer of general academic abilities (Blanton et al., 1995). Near-transfer studies investigated the transfer of skills and knowledge that the children had learned in the Fifth Dimension programs that were specific to the program. Examples of these included improvement in playing computer and board games (Study 1), factual knowledge of computers (Study 2), hands-on proficiency using computers (Study 3), and computer terminology (Study 4). In four studies, over time, students in the program showed improvement in playing computer and board games. Regarding improvement of factual knowledge of computers, students showed improvement in areas that they had been taught, and this was similar for the four near-transfer studies. These studies did not involve control groups.

Four studies explored the effects of Fifth Dimension on medium transfer of basic literacy skills to new tasks, investigating students' comprehension of computer game instructions. Two studies (Studies 5 and 6) were conducted at Appalachian State University in Boone, North Carolina, and at California State University, San Marcos. Another investigated the effects of the Fifth Dimension program on improving students' ease of learning to play a new math-related computer game. This study (Study 7) took place at the University of California at Santa Barbara. All the medium-transfer studies included control groups.

The students in Studies 5 and 6 were tested on an instrument that had been developed based on a specific computer game. All the students were administered the pretest, played the game once, and then were administered the posttest. Studies 5 and 6 showed differences in comprehension of instructions between the groups of students who had been involved in the program and those who had not.

Fifth Dimension is headquartered in California, with regional sites in Solano Beach, Escondido, La Jolla, and San Diego. The program exists at sites at 10 University of California campuses and also has sites in Boone, North Carolina, and Burlington, North Carolina. Fifth Dimension also has international sites in Sweden, Denmark, Russia, Israel, Mexico, and Australia.

The Imaginitis Learning System

The Imaginitis Learning System is a cooperative learning, afterschool, language arts program created for students in Grades 3-12. The goal of the program is to expose the participants to skills needed for effective and productive learning, in hopes that these will help the participants develop strong workplace competencies. The Imaginitis Learning System uses a language arts curriculum created at the University of Minnesota (Johnson & Johnson, 1996; Mitchell, 1996) to teach such skills as cooperation, team building, and conflict resolution.

When schools take on the Imaginitis Learning System, teachers are provided with a 1-day training program that emphasizes the principles of cooperative learning. Students in the program are divided into groups by age and grade and are provided with a task of working together in a team to creatively construct a book that eventually becomes a portfolio exhibition. The participants work individually on their own books as well as collectively as a team to create a finished class product. The team members work together and vote on what should be included or excluded in the process as well as in the final product. The teachers are trained to be coaches who keep scores based on the process of cooperative learning, as they observe the various teams engage in collaboration. These scores are taken into account at the end of the session when the teachers evaluate the final product. The teachers evaluate the end products for improvement of the students' writing, speaking, listening, and collaborating skills as well as for quality of the process that the students went through while planning the product.

The Imaginitis Learning System program has been evaluated in four sites across the country. The evaluations given to all the sites consisted of two parts. Students were asked to respond to two surveys that measured responses toward cooperative learning and working with others, mastering academic environments, and overall perceptions of student-teacher relationships. The second part of the evaluation measured the extent to which students reported that they would solve problems and resolve conflicts productively.

Four sites were used as test sites: Lynwood, California; Baltimore, Maryland; Philadelphia, Pennsylvania; and Washington, D.C. Overall, the results showed that Imaginitis students were significantly higher than control students in the areas of academic self-esteem, cooperation, and perceptions of student-teacher relationships. However, as with other afterschool programs, it was difficult to maintain a control group. In some cases, the groups were not evenly matched; in others, the groups were evenly matched, but the researchers were unable to gather data for all the sessions of the program. Because the Imaginitis students were self-selected, they cannot be considered evenly matched with control students, as the Imaginitis students were presumably more highly motivated. However, when the groups were evenly matched and the results were gathered for all sessions, Imaginitis students reported more positive results than non-Imaginitis students.

Overall, students who had been involved in Imaginitis the previous year were more likely to carry over the effects of the program the following year. This was the case in elementary schools and alternative high schools.

Explore Incorporated

Another extended-school-day program that attempts to improve students' academic achievement is Explore Incorporated (Explore Inc.). Explore Inc. has main themes incorporated in a curriculum written by academics in consultation with professionals in various academic fields. These themes include experiential learning, community service, physical education, homework support, and individual activities. As with other programs developed for similar purposes, Explore Inc. creates modular curriculum materials that are aligned with national, state, and district standards. Some of the curriculum modules include social studies (Community, Our Sense of Place), geography (One Earth, One Planet), entrepreneurship (Main Street Inc.), history (Time Traveler), life and biological sciences (Wildlife Discovery), computer science and literacy (Journey to the 21st Century), chemistry and physics (Invention Lab), visual and performing arts (Culture Club), leadership development (Trailblazers), and physical education and fitness (Young Olympians).

Using these themes and modules, Explore connects the goals of each lesson to state and national standards. The goal is to teach children to think critically, with expected outcomes being improved test scores.

When schools take on Explore Inc., the program hires certified teachers and community people (such as Scout leaders and community volunteers), who receive an initial, intensive training from Explore Inc. developers and trainers, followed by monthly monitoring and mini-inservices for the area directors. Explore Inc. also has family and community service components and provides children with homework assistance. Explore Inc. currently exists in in 30 schools in Massachusetts, Pennsylvania, New Jersey, and Maryland. No evaluation data are available.

Mindsurf

Mindsurf is an academic K-6 afterschool enrichment program created out of a partnership between National Geographic and Sylvan Learning Centers. The main goal of the program is to provide children with enriching academic achievement opportunities during the afterschool hours while at the same time creating safe and fun learning opportunities for the children. Children are engaged in the program between 3 p.m. and 6 p.m.

When schools take on Mindsurf, a certified teacher is trained to direct the program. The program director then employs additional teachers (usually certified) to lead and oversee the various activities that the children engage in while working on different themes, which are also referred to as clubs. When children enter the Mindsurf program, in addition to working on homework and study skills, they join various clubs of interest (thematic units), in which they work with other students and teachers using a 1:8 teacher-student ratio. The academic content of the Mindsurf program consists of various academic enrichment themes, such as Light and Color, Awesome Animals of North America, Storytelling, Australia, North America, Water, Blast Off, and Asia. These themes are explored using computers, camcorders, digital cameras, numerous software programs, and other innovative, advanced-technology pieces. In addition to participating in activities at learning centers, Mindsurf students receive individual kits that include activities for the children to engage in at home.

One of the newest components of Mindsurf is directed toward helping students improve their academic achievement. In addition to providing enrichment, Mindsurf attempts to provide some alignment with what happens during the day by encouraging and helping children complete their homework. This new development is referred to as the Surf Shop incentive program. In this program, students are trained to create assignment books that they use to log homework and then to complete this homework in the Mindsurf centers. They are also reinforced (with tokens) for neat homework completion and for showing good study skills habits.

Mindsurf currently serves 400 students in Maryland, Colorado, Washington, and California. No evaluation data are available.

Foundations Inc.

Foundations Inc. is an extended-school-day program for children in Grades K-12. Founded in 1992, the program brings together children, families, schools, and communities by providing children with academic enrichment programs on the school grounds during the nonschool hours.

When schools take on the program, they hire an on-site coordinator who is responsible for running the program as well as overseeing the staff. The school-level staff of Foundations Inc. programs consists of already certified teachers who have at least bachelor's degrees and sometimes master's degrees in education or other related fields, such as psychology, sociology, or social work. The educational staff members directly responsible for academic service delivery consists of certified academic tutors. All the teachers involved in the study are required to write lesson plans that provide detailed information about courses to be taught, learning goals and objectives, and results that they hope to attain. The community service component of Foundations Inc. also allows parents, community volunteers, and university students (sometimes interns) to volunteer their services in many capacities.

The curriculum strives to improve socioemotional, academic, and physical skills by teaching the students critical thinking, problem solving, social skills, good health, and safety. The main academic curriculum consists of five themes: All About Me (socioemotional unit), Our Global Festival (cultural and multicultural unit), On the Creative Express (creative units), Tech Quest, (study skills unit), and Action Earth (current events unit). This curriculum serves children in Grades K-8.

Foundations Inc. also has a young adolescents component that consists of afterschool activities and programs for middle school, junior high, and high school students. In addition to providing afterschool help, the program creates specialty clubs that help teenagers develop skills, hobbies, and interests in areas that are academic, recreational, and cultural. Some of these clubs include chess, dance, computers, business preparation, ceramics, karate, and photography.

Foundations Inc. underwent a small evaluation (Hamilton & Klein, 1998; Hamilton, Le, & Klein, 1999) that attempted to measure academic outcomes of Foundations Inc. students, using the Terra Nova Standardized Test. The study did not involve control and experimental groups and largely compared the Foundations Inc. group to a national norming sample. Very little information was provided on the demographics of the Foundations Inc. group, and so it is difficult to generalize these results, even pertaining to specific demographic samples. The results of the evaluation showed that Foundations Inc. students achieved higher test scores at the end of the program intervention. However, with no control group, it is hard to determine whether or not the academic gains were a result of participation in the program or not. Foundations Inc. is also engaged in a longer-term evaluation, and this should address the limitations of the pilot evaluation study. Foundations Inc. operates 20 programs and provides technical assistance to numerous programs across the country.

Summary

Table 3.1 presents a brief overview of categorizations of the enrichment afterschool programs reviewed in this chapter. All the programs reviewed were designed specifically for afterschool use and have an afterschool focus; four of the seven (Voyager, HOSO, Fifth Dimension, and Imaginitis) have been evaluated in afterschool settings; and only Fifth Dimension provides evidence of effectiveness; but a second program, Imaginitis, provides partial evidence. All the programs are academically oriented, which means that they aspire to attain some educational outcomes, yet few of them provide evidence of effectiveness. It is important to note that some of the programs reviewed may be too newly developed to provide any long-term evidence of effectiveness yet. Some of the programs (Voyager, Foundations) are engaged in rigorous evaluation research designs that will help in evaluating their effectiveness in the future, and others may or may not have intentions of engaging in such studies. As the various programs present themselves to consumers, it is important to generate questions about research and evidence of effectiveness in afterschool settings. This is especially true considering the amount of money that it takes to implement these programs. In the absence of evidence of effectiveness, schools, programs, and districts intending to adopt or implement these programs must be sure to investigate the extent to which the enrichments programs that they adopt are used to fulfill the needs of the particular populations that they are targeting.

Table 3.1　Categorization of Enrichment Afterschool Programs

Program Name	Grades Served	Afterschool Focus	Widely Replicated	Specially Designed for After School	Evaluated in Afterschool Settings	Evidence of Effectiveness After School	Academically Oriented
Voyager Expanded Learning	K-6	Yes	Yes	Yes	Yes	No	Yes
Hands On Science Outreach	Pre-K-6	Yes	Yes	Yes	Yes	No	Yes
Fifth Dimension	K-8	Yes	Yes	Yes	Yes	Yes	Yes/Partially
Imaginitis Learning System	3-12	Yes	Partially	Yes	Yes	Partial	Yes/Partially
Explore Inc.	K-8	Yes	Partially	Yes	No	No	Yes
Mindsurf	K-8	Yes	Partially	Yes	No	No	Yes
Foundations Inc.	K-12	Yes	Partially	Yes	No	No	Yes

4

Tutoring Programs to Improve
Reading and Study Skills Programs

his chapter is divided into two sections. The first section, adapted from
Wasik (1997), briefly addresses some structured tutoring programs that
exist either as afterschool programs or as in-school programs that could be
implemented during the afterschool hours. For more detailed information on
the programs, readers should refer to Wasik (1997) or contact the programs
listed in the appendix. Some of the programs selected for this review have evidence of effectiveness or evaluation, but some do not.

The second section addresses study skills programs. Study skills programs
can be useful to at-risk students whose academic skills suffer as a result of lack of
study skills. Two of the study skills programs included in this chapter (Study
Skills Across the Curriculum and Project IMPACT) do not provide specific curriculum content but do emphasize how to successfully organize and retain information taught in the classroom. This section describes two study skills programs that were not originally created as afterschool programs but can be used
for this purpose.

Howard Street Tutoring Program (HSTP)

The Howard Street Tutoring Program (Morris, 1990) is a remedial tutoring
program created for students in Grades 2 and 3 who are reading below grade
level.

When schools become involved in the HSTP, a reading specialist or reading
teacher becomes the on-site coordinator of the program. This person is trained
on how to tutor the students, how to write the lessons and lesson plans to be
used by the volunteers, and how to train the tutoring staff. As this is a volunteer
program, the staff consists of nonpaid adults and college students who must go
through the training program before they become tutors.

Classroom teachers, using an informal reading inventory, initially assess
potential student participants in the program. If the students are performing

significantly below grade level, they are placed in the program. Once enrolled, students engage in daily 1-hour one-to-one tutoring sessions, which take place every week.

The Howard Street program has been evaluated on a small scale. In two Chicago evaluations, HSTP students were randomly assigned to comparison groups and treatment groups. Students were assessed on word recognition (Harris & Jacobson, 1980), spelling (Schlagal, 1989), and basal passage reading. Results showed that students in the treatment groups outscored the students in the control groups on all the study measures and in all the areas: word recognition (ES = +.22) and basal word recognition (ES = +.59); spelling using a correct score (ES = +.56) and spelling using a qualitative score (ES = +.48); and basal passages (ES = +.99) (Morris, 1990; Morris, Shaw, & Perney, 1990).

Book Buddies

Book Buddies is a tutoring program created for first-grade students who have been identified by their classroom teachers as having reading problems. It was originally developed at the University of Virginia (Invernizzi, Juel, & Rosemary, 1996).

When schools take on the Book Buddies program, they hire an on-site program coordinator who is trained to implement the program. The tutorial training consists of 8 hours of initial training provided by the creators of the program and additional hours of training on an ongoing basis. The on-site coordinator is responsible for training and observing the tutors, who are mostly graduate students working on a master's degree or who have already earned a master's degree. The tutoring session is highly structured, and tutors are expected to follow the lessons prepared by the coordinator.

Once the students enroll in Book Buddies, they attend one-to-one tutoring sessions twice per week, in which they learn to read by rereading familiar storybooks, engaging in word study, and writing and reading new stories. The students use storybooks, a tutoring manual prepared with the help of the coordinators and the researchers, and other materials.

This program has not been evaluated in comparison to a control group. Book Buddies students who had received many sessions were compared with a group that had received fewer sessions. As would be expected, the group receiving more tutoring sessions did better. Many reasons (such as poor attendance) could explain why some students received fewer sessions, so this cannot be considered a conclusive evaluation. Book Buddies is currently used during the school day, but it could be adapted for use during the nonschool hours. Creators of Books Buddies are able and willing to train coordinators of afterschool programs to implement the program.

Help One Student To Succeed (HOSTS)

HOSTS (Gallegos, 1995; HOSTS Corporation, 1994; Wilbur, 1995) is a model that helps schools create tutoring programs for at-risk students using a mentoring approach. HOSTS schools provide one-to-one, usually afterschool, tutorial services to Title I students in elementary school through high school who are performing below the 30th percentile. This includes limited-English-proficient students and those who have been retained or are in special education classes. HOSTS trains volunteers from businesses and the community as well as peers and cross-age mentors, to serve as tutors.

HOSTS helps school staff members choose curriculum materials that are especially tailored to the individual needs of the children receiving services and aligned with what is being taught in the regular classroom. Schools involved in HOSTS have access to learning materials that have been specially designed to help the targeted population. The mentor or tutor follows a carefully designed lesson plan generated by the Title I teacher from a comprehensive database that aligns the curriculum of the schools to local objectives or state frameworks.

HOSTS evaluations have not included pre-post, experimental-control group comparisons. They have measured student success by looking at gains in national curve equivalent (NCE) scores, and the number of students who pass at grade level.

In a multistate study of HOSTS done for Title I national validation (HOSTS, 1994), students in Grades 1, 2, and 3 made substantial NCE spring-to-spring gains (15, 25, and 25, respectively), and students in other grades also made significant NCE gains. In a spring-to-spring California evaluation involving second, third, and fifth graders who were 95% Latino, the HOSTS students had NCE gains of 11.4, 9.5, and 9.9, respectively. These NCE gains exceeded those of the school and the state.

Since its inception in 1972 in Vancouver, Washington, HOSTS has involved over 150,000 students and 100,000 mentors in more than 4,000 programs nationwide, many of which are afterschool programs.

Reading Recovery With AmeriCorps

Reading Recovery With AmeriCorps is a variation of the original Reading Recovery tutoring program substantially adapted for use by volunteers. Whereas the original program (Clay, 1985; DeFord, Pinnell, Lyons, & Young, 1988; Huck & Pinnell, 1986; Pinnell, 1989; Pinnell, Lyons, DeFord, Bryk, & Seltzer, 1994; Pinnell, Short, Lyons, & Young, 1986; Wasik & Slavin, 1993) was designed for use only by certified reading tutors who are already credentialed teachers or reading specialists, the AmeriCorps version of the program trains community volunteers who are paid by AmeriCorps to deliver tutoring services to the students. As with the original Reading Recovery, this program is designed for students in Grade 1 who are reading below grade level.

Schools participating in the AmeriCorps/Reading Recovery program must already be Reading Recovery schools. The main overseer of the program is the Reading Recovery teacher, who is, of course, very familiar with the original Reading Recovery training program. This person provides AmeriCorps volunteers with 150 hours of initial training plus additional training and follow-up sessions. The Reading Recovery teacher and leader also provides the materials used in the program. Students are selected for the program based on identification by their classroom teachers. They are students with less severe reading problems who would not, therefore, meet the standard Reading Recovery criteria for tutoring services. Typically, the most at-risk children, those reading below the 20th percentile, would receive standard Reading Recovery tutoring from a certified teacher, whereas a less at-risk student would receive AmeriCorps volunteers as tutors. Once enrolled in the program, students receive one-to-one tutoring sessions every day. Some of the skills that the students learn include word knowledge, letter identification, concepts of print, text comprehension, and oral storybook reading.

Although the original Reading Recovery model has been evaluated many times using control groups, the AmeriCorps adaptation has not been evaluated in the same way. The research on AmeriCorps/Reading Recovery shows that students involved in the program made NCE gains, but it is not clear what gains they might have made without the program. Although AmeriCorps/Reading Recovery was mainly designed for use during school hours, it could be adapted for use during nonschool hours.

Intergenerational Reading Program (IRP)

This program was designed, using an intergenerational model, to improve the reading skills of first-grade students experiencing difficulties with reading. This program trains and sometimes pays senior citizens and foster grandparents as tutors.

When schools adopt the Intergenerational Reading Program, they hire a certified teacher who trains and supervises the volunteer tutors. The tutors are given three initial 3-hour training sessions in which they learn about metacognitive aspects of reading, such as graphophonemic relationships and phonics. In addition, tutors meet at least twice every month for continuing training.

Students who enter the program are first graders who are identified by their teachers as being at risk for reading problems. They receive one-to-one tutoring at least three times per week. The sessions consist of individualized tutoring sessions in which they learn basic elements of reading, such as phonics, spelling, and text in context, using storybooks and word strategy materials developed by the creators of the program.

The Intergenerational Reading Program is being evaluated, but there are as yet no data available.

Reading Together/VISTA

Reading Together/VISTA is an early intervention reading program designed for low-income kindergartners and pre-first-grade children (Neuman, 1995, 1996, 1997; Neuman & Gallagher, 1994; Neuman & Roskos, 1994, 1997; Roskos & Neuman, 1993; Shanahan & Neuman, 1997). The program is designed to expose young children to concepts of literacy and reading, using prop boxes to improve children's languages and skills. The prop boxes consist of a variety of articles put together to stimulate the use of new vocabulary and language among the children. Some of the contents include crayons, paper, pencils, interesting objects, and books.

Each Reading Together/VISTA school has a program coordinator. This person receives training on how to create, use, and train additional staff members to use the prop boxes. The staff consists mostly of trained VISTA volunteers, who then train parents of low-income children to work with their own children 2 hours per week. The VISTA staff members do not interact directly with the children; instead, they prepare and distribute the prop boxes and show parents how to use them with their children. In addition, they observe parents' interactions with their children and continuously provide feedback to the parents.

Students enrolled in the Reading Together/VISTA program do not have to be diagnosed as having reading problems prior to participation in the program. The goal of the program is to enrich the language arts experiences of the children before they enter first grade so that they will be less likely to be diagnosed as behind in reading or at risk for school failure.

A small evaluation of this program (Neuman, 1995) showed that students involved in the program made gains in reading when they entered first grade. This evaluation, however, did not include a control group.

Early Identification Program (EIP)

The Early Identification Program is an in-school program designed to improve students' reading performance in kindergarten. When schools enroll in the EIP program, they hire two part-time program coordinators who become responsible for the training of volunteer tutors. The initial training consists of teaching the tutors to use the tutoring manuals, which contain sequenced materials that students and tutors use. The staff that implements the tutoring program consists mainly of nonpaid community volunteers. Prospective EIP participants are identified by their kindergarten teachers.

Students in the EIP are provided with one-to-one tutoring sessions. These sessions focus on perceptual-motor and fine-motor skills, categorization concepts, and reading readiness skills.

The Early Identification Program was involved in an evaluation that compared EIP students with non-EIP students (EIP, 1989). Although the EIP students improved their scores, the nontutored group actually performed better than the tutored group on the tasks required of them. However, students were not randomly assigned to the groups, and those in the control group (less at risk) scored higher than the experimental group at the outset of the comparison.

Read Write Now!

Read Write Now! is a comprehensive effort to encourage children to enjoy reading in hopes of improving reading among at-risk youth before age nine (Riley 1995, 1996). The goal of Read Write Now! is to increase the amount of reading done by children (especially low-income children), and to encourage parents, volunteers, and teachers to participate in this process. Read Write Now! is not a specific method of tutoring but more a model that could be used to organize schools, cities, and local agencies (e.g., libraries) to set up tutoring programs for young children.

When schools or community centers participate in Read Write Now! the main person responsible for the administration of the program is a hired program coordinator. Read Write Now! does not require that the program coordinator be a certified teacher. This person then trains prospective tutors who are nonpaid parents and community volunteers. The tutors involved in the program receive training that is not necessarily uniform from site to site.

Unlike many of the other programs reviewed, Read Write Now! does not prediagnose students before they enter the program. Participation is open to everyone. It is more of a reading partners or reading buddies program than a tutoring program. The adult listens to children reading, providing minimum guidance when needed. Adults are encouraged to play positive roles in the lives of children by reading with them. The expected result of this program is that students will have a joy for reading and will progressively become better readers with increased opportunities to read.

Students engage in these activities at least once a week for 30 minutes and are encouraged to read the stories that they have already gone over from the materials provided. Students read storybooks mostly from their school and the public library.

The program does not have a prescribed method for teaching or training the tutors. Read Write Now! is basically an organizational effort providing information about some aspects of how to set up a reading buddies program.

Read Write Now! does not yet have evidence of effectiveness, but it is currently being evaluated formatively. Read Write Now! packages are available for schools, communities, and neighborhoods interested in implementing the program across the country. For a more extensive review of research on volunteer-tutoring programs, see Wasik, 1997.

Study Skills Across the Curriculum (SSAC)

Study Skills Across the Curriculum (1991) is a program designed for students in Grades 5-8 to improve their academic performance by learning study skills (Olson, 1993, 1995a, 1995b). Particularly, the program seeks to improve performance in content areas and to better prepare the students for active, independent, and successful learning in high school.

This program teaches students a variety of active learning strategies for studying and also teaches them how to prepare for different types of tests and examinations, such as multiple choice, true-false, essay, and short answer. Students are taught time management principles and strategies, SQ3R (a system for reading textbooks more efficiently), note taking from lectures and readings, semantic mapping, and additional study skills, such as underlining, highlighting, and listening skills.

When schools take on SSAC, a core group of representatives from the school receives training. This team typically consists of representatives from science, social studies, math, and English. The group then forms an implementation plan for the program to ensure the use of the study skills across the curriculum. In addition, parents are trained and encouraged to reinforce study skills when their children are engaged in homework activities.

This evaluation does not include evaluations of SSAC in afterschool settings. The evaluation of SSAC consisted of two parts. The first study compared the study skill patterns and performances of a group of 647 SSAC students to a group of 347 control students. Controlling for pretest differences, the SSAC students outperformed the control group on the study skills inventory (ES = +.52), which measured the extent to which different components of study skills taught in the program were used. The second part measured the performance of the students on a criterion-referenced study skills test created by the Study Skills program staff. Once again, the SSAC group students outscored the control group (ES = +2.76). However, the set of skills that were measured had not been taught to the control group.

The second part of the evaluation consisted of a comparison of academic report card grades earned by the students in the two groups at the end of the first and third quarters in English and science. Controlling for pretest differences, SSAC students outperformed the control students in English (ES = +.88) and science (ES = +.22).

Study Skills Across the Curriculum was not originally created for use in afterschool settings but has often been used in that way. The creators of the program are able and willing to help afterschool programs tailor SSAC to meet their needs. SSAC exists in 1,000 schools across the country.

Project IMPACT

Increasing Maximal Performance by Activating Critical Thinking (IMPACT) is a language arts and mathematics program that trains teachers to use critical thinking, problem solving, and higher-order thinking in mathematics and language arts with children in Grades 3-12 (Winocur, 1977). Project IMPACT was not designed for, but could be implemented in, afterschool settings.

With the help of Project IMPACT trainers, classroom teachers learn how to revise their current curriculum and include such critical thinking skills as inductive and deductive reasoning, problem solving, and decision making in their daily teaching. Implementation of the curriculum is self-monitored and peer-monitored, which involves other teachers, administrators, and project staff. Although the Project IMPACT curriculum was developed for use in mathematics and language arts, it has been expanded for implementation in science classes. Project IMPACT is used with high- and low-achieving students in urban, rural, suburban, public, and private schools.

Two evaluations of Project IMPACT have been done. These evaluations did *not* include the use of Project IMPACT in afterschool settings. The most recent evaluation compared IMPACT students in Grades 6-9 to matched students in a control group. The treatment students outperformed the control group on the Cornell Test of Critical Thinking with effect sizes of +1.81, +.64, +.42, and +.47 in Grades 6, 7, 8, and 9, respectively (Winocur, 1977).

Project IMPACT began in California and has been adopted by 480 public school districts, 2,384 public schools, and 124 private schools. The program now has adoption sites in 42 states in the United States plus Guam and Puerto Rico.

Summary

Table 4.1 categorizes 10 programs, 8 of which are volunteer tutoring programs and 2 of which are study skills programs. In 1996, when the Read Write Now! initiative was created, many afterschool programs were in search of programs that would help enhance and improve reading. At the time, the U. S. president and secretary of education's Read Write Now! initiative sounded catching, in that it included using voluntary tutors as instructors to teach reading in the afterschool program. This seemed like a wonderful idea and a solution to the "reading by 9" issue that was a hot topic at the time. Wasik (1997) embarked on a national review of volunteer tutoring programs and found that very few showed evidence of effectiveness in afterschool settings. This chapter reviewed some of these programs and basically reaches a similar conclusion. It is impossible to attain positive results in education without hiring and training qualified staff. Of the eight volunteer tutoring programs reviewed in this chapter, only three have provided *any* evidence of effectiveness in afterschool settings.

Table 4.1   Categorization of Volunteer Tutoring and Study Skills Programs

Program Name	Grades Served	Afterschool Focus	Widely Replicated	Specially Designed for After School	Evaluated in Afterschool Settings	Evidence of Effectiveness After School	Academically Oriented
Volunteer Tutoring Programs							
Howard Street Tutoring Program	2-3	Yes	Yes	Yes	Yes	Yes	Yes
Book Buddies	1	Yes	Yes	No	Yes	Partial	Yes
HOSTS	K-6	Yes	Yes	Yes	Yes	Yes	Yes
Reading Recovery With Americorps	1	Yes	Yes	Yes	No	No	Yes
Intergenerational Reading Program	1	Yes	Partially	No	No	No	Yes
Reading Together/VISTA	K	Yes	Yes	No	No	No	Yes
Early Identification Program	K	Yes	Partially	No	No	No	Yes
Read Write Now!	K-3	Yes	Yes	Yes	No	No	Yes
Study Skills Programs							
Study Skills Across the Curriculum	5-8	Yes	Yes	No	No	No	Yes
Project IMPACT	3-12	Yes	Yes	No	No	No	Yes

5

Community-Based
Afterschool Programs

This chapter discusses programs that were created for use primarily in afterschool settings that have a community focus. Some of the programs in this section are offered in schools and others in community buildings.

New York City Beacons

In 1991, the New York City Department of Youth and Community Development created the New York City Beacons program in 10 schools (Canada, 1996; Lakes, 1996; McGillis, 1996). The main goal of the program is to reduce crime and violence among youth and their families by providing afterschool programs for the whole family, to ultimately improve school and community linkages. By improving parental participation in the lives of the children, the program was intended to lead to better and more supportive neighborhoods for children, youth, and families.

The Beacons are school-based community programs, which means that they are located in schools but also serve school-age children living within the area who do not attend the schools in which the programs are operated. The programs provide a combination of educational, cultural, and recreational programs for all the community participants. Students can participate in cultural and recreational programs, such as Boy Scouts, Girl Scouts, seasonal sports, and Boys & Girls Clubs, and they can enroll in other cultural and recreational programs that specifically fit the needs and desires of the communities the families live in. In addition to providing afterschool programs in the individual school sites, Beacons programs provide family services such as Adult Basic Education, English as a Second Language (ESL), Family Counseling, Parent Education, and a range of health and social services on site. They also serve as venues for community meetings.

The Beacons afterschool programs for youth also stress academic support, remediation, and enrichment. Examples of academic assistance include tutoring, homework help, SAT and ACT preparation, and college preparatory classes. All the Beacons schools are also regularly involved in technical assistance programs with the Fund for the City of New York. For example, the Beacons have an educational curriculum and training component titled Making Literacy Links, which focuses on literacy and uses journal writing, storytelling, and reading activities. Enrichment activities include video production, newspaper production, and script writing.

When schools become Beacons, they are required to maintain a Community Advisory Council, which must include teachers, parents, principals, youth neighborhood organizations, and other community residents. The Council continuously oversees the various entities involved in the group and ensures that they all contribute to the progress and cohesiveness of the program. The lead agencies, usually existing community agencies, recruit and provide services to the members. The lead agencies generally stay open longer hours, already exist in the community, and are already ethnically, racially, and culturally sensitive to the needs of the communities they serve.

The Beacons have four main goals: youth development, parental involvement and family support, school-home-community linkages, and building safe and supportive neighborhoods for child and youth development.

The youth development aspect of the program aims to provide students with a sense of community. Youth are engaged in challenging and engaging activities that allow them to participate meaningfully in decision making, with a goal of eliminating such challenges to teenagers as violence, substance abuse, juvenile delinquency, and teenage pregnancy.

The improved school-home-community linkages strive to use the school as an educational forum that changes and forms the community into a goal-oriented network of youth and adults, school staff members, schools as a whole, and minority communities. Some of the goals of these linkages include increasing school attendance and improving community problem-solving capabilities. The schools and the Department of Youth and Community Development also collaborate with the Administration for Children's Services to provide additional social services for the children involved in the Beacons program.

Parental involvement in the Beacons program includes getting parents to help in the afterschool program and offering opportunities for the adults to improve themselves through adult education, cultural, and recreation classes during the nonschool hours. As they strive to improve relations between schools and parents, the Beacons staff members help parents by accompanying them to meetings with school staff and by hosting parent-teacher Beacons meetings.

Beacons programs exist in 40 New York City schools and are currently undergoing an evaluation.

LA's BEST

Los Angeles's Better Educated Students for Tomorrow (LA's BEST) is an afterschool, education and enrichment program created in 1988 for students in Los Angeles (Brooks & Herman, 1991; Huang, Gribbons, Kim, Lee, & Baker, 2000). The goals of the program are to create a safe environment for students living in the city; to provide students with enhanced educational, enrichment, and recreational activities; and to teach socioemotional skills. LA's BEST currently serves about 5,000 students at 24 elementary schools in the Los Angeles Unified School District.

To become an LA's BEST school, the site must have students who are academically challenged (low test scores) and financially disadvantaged, and must be located in a high crime neighborhood in the Los Angeles Unified School District. The main overseer of each local school program is the site coordinator (some sites may have more than one). By design, each site coordinator is given a great deal of local autonomy. This person also oversees additional staff members—program supervisors, playground workers, specialized small-group leaders, high school student workers, and volunteers. All employees of LA's BEST are qualified by the Los Angeles Unified School District. Although the basic minimum requirements for the positions are only fingerprints, clearance, and TB tests, the site coordinators and program supervisors tend to be teachers from the regular school day who are credentialed. The program hopes to reach students who are challenged academically, socially, and socioemotionally and deter them from violence and crime by providing them with homework assistance; academic enrichment; cultural and recreational experiences; development of talents, skills, and hobbies; socioemotional support; and enrichment opportunities, such as theater and visual arts and monthly field trips. LA's BEST involves the local school community and community persons in the development, running, and organization of the program by hiring high school students and college undergraduates as well as community and neighborhood residents to serve as aides, and by providing parents with opportunities to volunteer.

When students enroll in LA's BEST, they initially participate in the basic academic program, which provides them with opportunities to improve their skills in areas in which they may need help. All the LA's BEST students are required to participate in the homework lab, in which students are tutored by aides and other members of the staff in reading, language arts, mathematics, and other subjects. The tutors, who are responsible for academic tutoring in the homework labs in LA's BEST, have regular training in the varying ways that children learn, and they are supported by supervisors, activity consultants, a full-time program director, and the president and CEO. Other required academic activities for all LA's BEST participants include computer skills and literacy development, and these activities take place every day. In addition to the required academic activities, other academic enrichment clubs and opportunities include, but are not limited to, science and mathematics clubs. After the academic period, students choose from a variety of recreational, cultural, and enrichment activities. LA's BEST is offered at no cost to parents on a first-come, first-served basis. Students must maintain minimal attendance (which varies from site to site) or they may lose their place in the program to other students on waiting lists.

LA's BEST also encourages parents to attend family-oriented, citywide events. The events are combinations of fun activities and workshops for the families (especially for parents or guardians) on parenting issues. The goal of these events is to familiarize parents with issues pertaining to the schooling of their children, so they will eventually become more involved.

The first evaluation of LA's BEST was a formative evaluation of the program (Brooks & Herman, 1991). Surveys were given to parents, staff, and children. Parents and students felt that they had benefited from the program. The evaluators advised that future evaluations should include more rigorous qualitative and quantitative evaluations.

Since the original evaluation, a longitudinal, formative and summative evaluation of the program was performed by the Center for the Study of Evaluation at UCLA (Brooks, Mojica, & Land, 1995). This evaluation was a longitudinal study of the effects of LA's BEST on children's academic skills, parents, and students' motivation to succeed in school.

This study was a matched-comparison design. The study involved 80 fifth- and sixth-grade LA's BEST students and 66 fifth- and sixth-grade students in the comparison group. Students were selected for the treatment or comparison group on the basis of availability, number of years enrolled in the program, and parental permission to participate in the study. The study compared the grades of students who participated in LA's BEST for 2 years with those of students who participated for at most 3 months and then left the program. The students were not equal in the beginning, but using statistical procedures to control for outliers, the two groups were slightly more comparable. At the onset of the evaluation, students in the control group outscored students in the experimental group in the areas of mathematics, science, social studies, and composition and were higher in reading. At the end of the study, grades and effort scores of students in both groups increased. Scores of the LA's BEST students increased more than those of the students in the control group, and they even outscored them in all areas in the end. However, only the differences in reading scores between the two groups were statistically significant in 1991 and 1992 ($p < .05$).

Additional evaluations of LA's BEST included interviews with the students about their environments and issues related to safety and availability of helpful resources during the nonschool hours. Students who attended LA's BEST answered that they felt safer during the afterschool hours, had more access to helpful resources, liked school more, had higher aspirations to complete high school, and were less likely to participate in gangs. Finally, parent interviews revealed that parents felt that students were in a safe environment and that they were being encouraged to apply themselves academically.

One should interpret the findings of this evaluation with caution. Although the difference between the two groups was significant for reading scores, selection bias is a factor in this evaluation and is an issue that the evaluators also address (Brooks et al., 1995). Participation in LA's BEST requires parental permission, regular attendance in the program, willingness to participate in the program, and a host of other factors that already distinguish participants in the program from nonparticipants. The evaluators also mentioned that there were specific demographic differences between the two groups of students, such as availability of care, different grades for the comparison group, more parents of the comparison group speaking English as a second language, and more parents of the comparison group being unemployed. Looking at these factors, even when there were some significant results and favorable patterns for students involved in the program, it would indeed be difficult to conclude that the differences in grades, academic effort, and feelings of safety were caused by the LA's BEST program alone.

Child First Authority (CFA)

The Child First Authority is a Baltimore community-based afterschool program that seeks to improve the quality of life in low socioeconomic-status communities. The CFA received funding from the mayor's office, the governor, and the city council through a local Industrial Areas Foundation branch named Baltimoreans United in Leadership Development (BUILD) in the summer of 1996. During the first year of funding, the CFA established community-based learning centers in 10 schools. The main goal of this program is to improve the quality of life in Baltimore City by directly serving public school students and their families academically, culturally, and behaviorally in the school-based, extended-day centers. The program uses the schools as hubs of activity in which parents, staff members, administrators, church members, students, and other community members get together. Although the overall goal of the program is the improvement of the quality of life, the CFA programs in the schools in Baltimore are not all the same. BUILD oversees the program as a whole and specifies the parent and community components of the program, but the programs have evolved differently from site to site. For example, different extended-school-day centers have chosen to use different cultural enrichment programs, depending on the needs and the goals of the program planning teams.

Similar to LA's BEST and the Beacons program, Child First seeks to tie parents and communities together. The CFA Advisory Board, made up of representatives from BUILD, the mayor's office, and the city council, meets monthly. In addition, each site has a planning team made up of community, school, and church entities. This team determines the content and structure of each program at each site and votes on all policy issues that the programs take on.

To become a Child First school, a school must be identified by a BUILD member, who then engages in discussions with the principal to determine if the school is ready to take on the responsibilities involved. A school planning team then signs a compact with the organizing body, which grants the group access to the school, access to the parents, and space for the afterschool program.

Each school employs a program coordinator, an academic coordinator, and a parent volunteer coordinator. The academic parts of the program function as true extended-school-day programs, which means that the teachers who work during the regular school day are the academic teachers in the afterschool hours and are trained in teaching reading, writing, language arts, and other subjects. Some of the programs incorporate externally developed, extended-school-day programs that are taught by the regular school-day teachers.

The main evaluation of the CFA consists of a historical account of the program during the first year, which is in the form of a formative evaluation (Fashola, 1999, in press). Currently, the CFA is undergoing a summative evaluation of the third year of the program. This evaluation will provide outcome information about the impact of the CFA on grades, school attendance, and parental participation of CFA students as compared to non-CFA participants in the specific schools, and in the district overall.

Big Brothers Big Sisters of America

Big Brothers Big Sisters of America was created specifically to provide young children from single-parent families with adult mentors. The organization is mainly funded by the U.S. Department of Justice. The goal of this program is to provide young children (especially inner-city children and children from single-parent homes) with role models in their everyday lives who will provide them with positive experiences, teach them to make healthy decisions, and help them strive for the best in life.

Children participate in Big Brothers Big Sisters by connecting with local agencies, but there is a waiting list. Adults who sign up to be Big Brothers and Big Sisters are screened and, if selected, asked to spend at least 4 to 6 hours every month with their little brothers or sisters.

A randomized evaluation study of the program was performed to investigate the effects on youth who had been provided with services compared to youth who had not been provided with services (Tierney & Grossman, 2000). In this study, 959 children (ages 10-16) who had applied to be a part of the Big Brothers Big Sisters program were randomly assigned to a treatment group (487 participants) or a waiting list, which served as a control group (472 participants) for 18 months. Results showed that students who were a part of the study were significantly less likely to start using drugs and alcohol or engage in aggressive activities and more likely to improve school performance and attendance and improve their peer relationships. Evaluations of the study have shown that both adults and children have enjoyed being in the program. Recently, the Department of Justice granted agencies across the country additional funding, based on evidence that such programs have reduced violence, pregnancy, and unwanted behaviors among inner-city youth.

Boy Scouts of America (BSA)

The Boy Scouts is one of the oldest youth organizations in the world. The program seeks to enrich the lives of young males and teach them how to become model citizens by providing them with educational, mentoring, social, cultural, and recreational opportunities and activities on a regular basis. Any organization can begin a Boy Scout troop. Boy Scout troops currently exist in churches, schools, afterschool programs, recreational centers, community centers, and other entities. The youngest age of participation for children is 7, and Scouting can continue into adulthood.

Girl Scouts of the USA (GSUSA)

A sister organization to the BSA is the Girl Scouts, created by Juliette Gordon Low in 1912. The goal of this organization is to provide girls with enrichment: educational, recreational, and cultural opportunities that will help them develop into positive and productive citizens. The GSUSA is the oldest and most comprehensive organization that provides such opportunities for girls. Any organization can begin a Girl Scout troop in a church, school, afterschool or in-school program, recreational center, community center, and so forth. Girl Scouts offers different levels of membership geared toward different age groups.

The youngest GSUSA group is Daisy Scouts for children in K-1, and participation can continue into adulthood.

Camp Fire Boys and Girls

The Camp Fire Boys and Girls organization teaches youth about the dangers and the safeties of camping outdoors. This organization began in 1910 as an educational attempt to teach youth about the dangers of forest fires and how to prevent them. Programs have the option of adding an environmental component to their afterschool or extended-school-day programs.

With a strong history of promoting and encouraging positive youth development, Camp Fire Boys and Girls provides children and youth across the United States with an understanding of the role of community service in their lives. Programs provide the opportunities to translate that understanding into action through partnerships with families, schools, peers, and communities. Specifically, Camp Fire's child care, club (small groups of youth working with adult mentors), and camping programs provide quality out-of-school experiences for children and youth. Some of these experiences include citizenship, appreciation for volunteerism, decision making, fostering inclusiveness, and empowerment.

The guiding purpose of Camp Fire is, through a program of informal education, to provide young people with a range of opportunities for skill development and for self and social development. The goal is to maximize their potential and function effectively as caring, self-directed individuals responsible to themselves and others.

4-H

The 4-H program was begun at the turn of the 20th century in response to a need to introduce youth to nature study as a basis for better agricultural education. The 4-Hs are *head* (training youth to think, plan, and reason), *heart* (training youth to be true, kind, and sympathetic), *hands* (training youth to be useful, helpful, and skillful), and *health* (training youth to develop health and vitality). The program is generally funded by the U.S. Department of Agriculture (USDA) through local land-grant universities and sometimes through city agencies. Most of the 4-H headquarters are stationed at universities in departments that emphasize agriculture and education.

The 4-H program has not been evaluated for its effects on academic achievement of the students, but it has explored the effects of the program on the positive use of unstructured time. A survey of 114 participants (Fleming-McCormick & Tushnet, 1996) explored the effects of the 4-H program on self concept, aversion to negative peer groups, problem solving, and positive attitudes toward school work. Sixty-two participants responded to the study; the majority of the respondents stated that they had been involved in gangs prior to participation in the program and that the program helped to keep them out of gangs. Interviews with parents and teachers of the students also reported better problem solving, more interest in school work, better attitudes toward school work, and more enthusiasm toward learning.

These results, although positive, are not conclusive about the results of 4-H. As with many other programs, there are no control groups, and the information provided is based solely on surveys of respondents who chose to respond. Again, self-selection is the biggest problem of this study. It is difficult to generalize whether the program had the same effect on the majority of the 4-H participants or why some students and not others reported these results.

Schools wishing to incorporate 4-H components into their programs may contact their local 4-H offices. Complete curricula are offered by 4-H, along with guides and manuals for implementation, and the 4-H council has evaluated these curricula. The 4-H clubs also have community service and work-training components that they incorporate into their programs. They have ready-to-go kits available for teaching various topics, which can be obtained by telephone, letter, or e-mail.

Boys & Girls Clubs of America

Boys & Girls Clubs of America comprises a national network of more than 2,000 neighborhood-based facilities annually serving some 2.8 million young people, primarily from disadvantaged circumstances. Known as "The Positive Place for Kids," the clubs provide guidance-oriented character development programs on a daily basis for children 6-18 years old, conducted by a full-time, trained, professional staff. Boys & Girls Clubs programs emphasize educational achievement, career exploration, drug and alcohol prevention and avoidance, health and fitness, gang and violence prevention, cultural enrichment, leadership development, and community service.

Boys & Girls Club programs were also developed to provide youth with safe havens during the nonschool hours. In addition, the programs provide fairly structured environments, in which young children receive homework help, some academic classes, opportunities to use computers, and other recreational opportunities. Boys & Girls Clubs also allow children to develop cultural and recreational skills, through teaching drama, dance, and club sports such as basketball, volleyball, football, and soccer. Boys & Girls Clubs exist all over the country in both rural and urban neighborhoods. Boys & Girls Clubs and schools may choose to collaborate during the nonschool hours to widen the scope of their services.

Police Athletic League (PAL)

The Police Athletic League is an afterschool service-providing program begun as an effort to reduce violence and delinquency among inner-city youth. The program strives to improve relations between inner-city youth and the police and to provide youth with safe havens in the community by providing community service officers to act as tutors, mentors, teachers, and role models in PAL centers. The first PAL center was begun in Chicago; there are now centers in many cities across the United States. Similar to other afterschool programs, PAL programs offer homework help, arts and crafts, and recreational activities. PAL stresses educational excellence among its participants by keeping close track of attendance records. The Police Athletic League program is most well known for its athletic component. Students enrolled in the program have opportunities to try out for and compete in sports like volleyball, soccer, basketball, and football, and the league sponsors these programs.

The preliminary results of evaluations of PAL show reductions in juvenile deliquency (Baltimore Police Department Division of Planning and Research, 1998).

Summary

Table 5.1 presents a summary of community-based programs offering afterschool programs to children. This category of programs is especially important because such programs serve large volumes of children in need of afterschool programs. Such centers exist all over the country, serving both rural and urban populations. The community-based programs have good intentions and serve a variety of students, but many do not have the infrastructure needed for rigorous and robust evaluation. All the programs have an afterschool focus, and most are widely replicated, yet only two provide evidence of effectiveness during the afterschool hours (Big Brothers Big Sisters of America and LA's BEST). Surely, if the programs want to see their impact on the populations they serve, they will benefit from creating infrastructures that facilitate rigorous evaluations.

What is promising is that, as a result of the efforts of the 21st Century Community Center's task force on evaluation, many community-based and school-based afterschool programs and evaluators are engaging in continuous dialogue about the importance and feasibility of important evaluation. The next two chapters discuss not only the importance of evaluation but also how to create and conduct evaluations of afterschool programs.

Table 5.1   Categorization of Community-Based Afterschool Programs

Program Name	Grades Served	Afterschool Focus	Widely Replicated	Specially Designed for After School	Evaluated in Afterschool Settings	Evidence of Effectiveness After School	Academically Oriented
New York City Beacons	K-12	Yes	Yes	Yes	No	No	Yes/Partially
LA's BEST	K-12	Yes	Yes	Yes	Yes	Partial	Yes/Partially
Child First Authority	K-12	Yes	No	Yes	No	No	Partially
Big Brothers Big Sisters of America	K-12	Yes	Yes	Partially	Yes	Yes	Partially
Boy Scouts of America	K-12	Yes	Yes	Partially	No	No	Partially
Girls Scouts of the USA	K-12	Yes	Yes	Partially	No	No	Partially
Camp Fire Boys and Girls	K-12	Yes	Yes	Partially	No	No	Partially
4-H	K-12	Yes	Yes	Partially	No	No	Partially
Boys & Girls Clubs	K-12	Yes	Yes	Partially	No	No	Partially
Police Athletic League	K-12	Yes	Yes	Partially	No	No	Partially

55

6

How to Create an Afterschool Program: From Conception to Implementation

The first section of this book discussed existing programs that can possibly enhance and improve afterschool programs. This is assuming that the programs mentioned are already operating and are interested in finding out about the other programs that they could collaborate with and afford. Today, however, afterschool programs are beginning with nothing and are interested in finding out how to create their own programs from the beginning. This chapter addresses creating an afterschool program from conception to implementation and provides an overview of important topics to consider when doing this.

Many teachers and administrators may wish to run afterschool programs but may lack information on how to go about creating them, whom to include in the programs, what components to add to the program, and, also, how to run and implement the program. This chapter addresses these concerns by discussing topics such as creating and conducting a needs assessment, creating the afterschool committees and setting goals, creating the various components of the afterschool program, and, finally, training the service providers in the afterschool programs.

Assessing the Situation

* Tools of instruments

Creating and Conducting a Needs Assessment

The needs assessment is the first data tool to be used in the creation of afterschool programs. A needs assessment is a general evaluation tool that could take the form of individual interviews, surveys, focus groups, town and community meetings, parental organizational meetings, and so forth. The needs assessment is a tool that helps identify the voids in services in the community but also the ways in which these voids could possibly be filled by creating a custom-made, afterschool program that will fulfill the needs of all the players. The ultimate goal of this assessment is to establish whether or not there is a need to create or establish an afterschool program.

For example, if the main concerns of the community are violence and juvenile delinquency, then through various group meetings or needs assessment sessions, the proponents of afterschool programs should seek to find ways to meet the needs of the community by providing an afterschool program that has as its main goal reduction of violence and juvenile delinquency. As another example, while the needs assessment is being conducted, the community might conclude that children's afterschool safety is a large topic of concern and that the best type of space that would benefit the program would be the local public school building, in which students will always be under the supervision of professional teachers. Using a public school building would help solve safety concerns.

Following this example, the school administrator might be willing to provide the school building for an afterschool program but may have prioritized the needs of the afterschool program differently. The principal might express a greater need for an academically based afterschool program that will help enhance and enrich the academic achievement of the students. If the needs assessment yields results that show no need for an afterschool program, then schools and community programs may have to be more creative in convincing the groups that such a program will be fruitful for them.

When the program is created using the needs assessment results, and the entities that expressed needs are involved in creating the program, then all the partners and participators feel a sense of ownership. This sense of ownership is one of the factors that will eventually sustain the program in the future. Once the needs assessment has been distributed and analyzed, the next step is to form committees that will establish specific goals for the program.

Assessing the Results: Involving All Parties

The goals of an afterschool program determine the makeup, content, and outcomes of the program. The extent to which the goals are set with precision and accuracy determines the extent to which the program will serve the needy populations correctly and, eventually, engage in effective evaluations. Once the needs assessment has been conducted, the group should examine the results and collectively establish priorities. These priorities should reflect the needs of the students, parents, community, school, and any other entities or stakeholders involved. This is important because each of these subsets of stakeholders has a specific and important role to play in the success of the program. If one of the groups of people is not included, then the success of the program is at stake.

For example, a program might decide to create a well-rounded, afterschool program and set the hours of the program from 2:30 p.m. to 5 p.m., but forget to consult with the parents of the students. This could be a problem because of the hours of operation. Parents may like the program and actually be in need of the services, but the hours of operation could be a hindrance to the participation of the students. Involving parents in the goals by setting sessions that address stakeholders' wants, needs, and concerns would encourage the program to address transportation issues by either extending the hours of the program or by providing some transportation options for the participants.

Creating the Committees and Executing Goals

There is a lot of work involved in creating and executing program goals. This cannot be the responsibility of one person alone, as it will become overwhelming. One option is to create various committees that are directly responsible for making sure that the goals will be well executed. The responsibilities of the goals committees are to clarify the goals, make them concrete, and execute them. This committee actually works closely with the evaluation committee, as those goals that are set are those that will eventually be evaluated. The goals committee should work hand in hand with the evaluation committee to measure the intermediate milestones prior to the end-of-year evaluations.

The goals committee should create small subcommittees whose responsibility is to take on an individual goal or two and investigate means to execute these goals. Capable persons who are trained in the area of the goal to be implemented should head the committees. For example, if one of the goals was to improve the reading skills of the students, the academics committee—headed by a staff member with training in the area of reading programs—would be responsible for the curriculum, materials, and training of other staff members. Some examples of committees that are dedicated to the implementation of specific goals include academics, recreation, cultural, training, and administration. Other committees could be in charge of such issues as orientation, volunteer involvement, materials, and scheduling. These various committees should be responsible for, and be able to answer questions pertaining to, these various areas of the afterschool program.

Creating the Components

Although afterschool programs are highly diverse in purpose, funding, and quality, most of them face a common set of implementation issues. For example, decisions must be made about who will attend the program, what to do if children attend irregularly or drop out, how to obtain funding to continue the program once the current source of funding expires, and how to recruit, train, and sustain paid staff and volunteers. If the various committees are able to envision the type of program that they wish to operate, then the various committees should create their components. The next section addresses the components of an afterschool program.

Bronfenbrenner (1986), in his ecological approach to the study of the development of the "whole" child, has shown that community, family, school, and friends have a great deal of influence on what happens to the child in school as well as out of school. If these external forces are supportive of what takes place during the day (and vice versa), then the academic, emotional, and social development of the child are more likely to complement one another and lead to the healthy development of the whole child. If any of the external forces are not in harmony, it is more difficult to attain this goal. Time after school is prime for the implementation of programs to complement, enhance, and enrich what happens during the regular school day. Effective extended-school-day and afterschool programs are capable of addressing three developmental needs of the whole child: academic, recreational, and cultural. The next section provides brief descriptions of these program components.

The Academic Component

Many afterschool programs offer academic services to the students involved, regardless of where they are located. A carefully planned and executed academic component of an afterschool program is one way to ensure success, but this is not guaranteed if quality materials and well-trained staff members are not used. The school or community center must decide whether the goal of its academic component is to improve the school-day performance of children through activities tied to the school curriculum, through enrichment activities, or through both. If the academic program is directly connected to what happens during the school day, then curriculum planners must be more selective with what they choose to teach and to carefully align the afterschool curriculum with school curricula and objectives. Academic subjects taught during the afterschool period require qualified, preferably certified, instructors, who are familiar with, and can be held accountable for, student outcomes.

If the afterschool program is implementing remedial programs to supplement what is being taught during the day, key decisions must be made. Will the same program be used during the school and afterschool instruction, or will a separate afterschool program be effective? Whatever the decision, the staff members must be trained to implement the program effectively, and care must be taken to ensure that the school-day and afterschool curriculum materials are aligned.

One of the most efficient ways to ensure curricular alignment is to staff academically based extended-day and afterschool classes with effective classroom teachers who are already familiar with the curriculum plans and objectives. This is, of course, much easier to do in an extended-day program that operates in the same school building. However, even in a traditional afterschool program in a community center, it is possible to maintain a degree of curricular alignment by providing homework assistance and activities that promote basic skills learning. One the other hand, it could also be difficult to recruit, train, and pay teachers to stay an extra few hours every day. Some of the staff members may be tired after a full day's work, and others may simply not be interested. In other cases, it may also be difficult for the teaching staff to differentiate between academics taught during the regular school day and academics taught in the afternoon. Training sessions are one good avenue to use to resolve these potential difficulties before they arise.

Creating a Structured Academic Program. Over the past few years, researchers (e.g., Pierce, Hamm, & Vandell, 1997; Posner & Vandell, 1994) have shown that when the goal of an afterschool program is to enhance academic achievement, structure is essential. Reviews of research on effective school programs (Block, Everson, & Guskey, 1995; Fashola & Slavin, 1997, 1998a 1998b; Slavin & Fashola, 1998; Slavin, Karweit, & Madden 1989; Slavin, Karweit, & Wasik, 1994) show that successful academic programs have usually had clear goals, well-developed procedures for attaining those goals, and extensive professional development. Similarly, academically oriented programs implemented during the nonschool hours need to adopt or create well-structured programs that provide extensive training. Many of the programs in this review—such as Voyager, Junior Great Books, Books and Beyond, and Project Success Enrichment—have relatively structured materials and training procedures. This is not to say that all afterschool programs must implement prepackaged academic programs from outside vendors. However, if a school plans or chooses to create and implement its own program, time must be put aside for structural and component planning, curriculum development, and training.

The Recreational Component

Once the academic goals for the day have been fulfilled, recreational aspects of the development of the whole child can be worked on during the remaining time of the afterschool day (Pointsett, 1996). In the past, many children grew up involved in extracurricular activities such as Little League baseball or softball in their neighborhood parks or on school fields. Evening and Saturday Little League games provided the children with opportunities to play organized sports and develop social skills and values such as teamwork, good sportsmanship, coping strategies, and problem solving. In addition, the Little League coach often served as a role model for many of the children. Also, students often had opportunities to participate in drama, music, chess clubs, science clubs, and other activities during the afterschool hours.

Because extended-school-day programs almost always serve smaller numbers of children than the school as a whole, they can make effective use of resources that are less easily available during the school day. For example, a limited number of computers can serve the needs of afterschool computer clubs, because there are smaller student-to-computer ratios. One small stage can meet the needs of a drama club because there are fewer students enrolled in the class. Also, volunteers willing to work with children on academic, cultural, or sports activities, especially older students, are usually more available after school than during school.

Today, many inner-city neighborhood parks are drug infested or otherwise unsafe for young children to play in. School and community budgets have been cut, and physical activities, clubs, and recreational experiences have become limited. The extended-school-day period provides schools with an opportunity to bring recreational activities back to the children who need them the most. For example, Posner and Vandell (1994) note that "unless they participated in an afterschool program, enrichment lessons such as music and dance were not a part of the lives of these low-income children, nor did the children engage in team sports to a significant extent" (p. 25).

The recreational portion of the program can provide the children with opportunities to develop whatever skills they choose. To develop their talents fully, additional hands-on encounters with areas of enrichment should be given to the children on a regular basis. For example, an urban youth who has expressed an interest in outdoor life could be invited to participate in an outdoor hiking event sponsored by a club or by a person who has taken an interest in exposing youth to such events. Although exposing this child to the event may be an enriching and stimulating experience, an isolated encounter will not develop the talents that the student would need to be an avid hiker. Although a singular opportunity may foster a child's interest in a particular activity, further experiences must be offered for students to explore in-depth their interests.

In a separate example, students who are interested in computers may tour a university's computing facilities and be exposed to the uses of computers in various settings. Once again, this one-time experience is insufficient to develop the talents of the students in the areas of computers and computer technology. Well-intended, onetime exposure events are not enough to provide enriching academic or recreational opportunities for the children. Afterschool or extended-school-day programs could provide social and cultural activities and additional opportunities by creating clubs, scheduling classes, and creating activities that will develop the talents of the children and improve opportunities for both expert and novice activities. Creating clubs that allow opportunities for talent development is an endeavor that has been beneficial to youth in all communities, especially if they are well developed, goal oriented, and have been evaluated for evidence of effectiveness. Some organizations that offer such opportunities include Boy Scouts, Girl Scouts, the YMCA and YWCA, 4-H, Camp Fire Boys and Girls, and Boys & Girls Clubs of America, and they are described in previous chapters. These organizations provide opportunities for rural and urban young children to be introduced to new skills and to develop new talents that they would not ordinarily be able to cultivate. Programs like 4-H, Scouting, and Camp Fire Boys and Girls have various levels of skill and talent development that are tailored developmentally to the age levels of participants. The goals of such programs are to enrich and expand the opportunities of all children by exposing them to a variety of activities. If these programs are implemented in schools and communities during the nonschool hours, the fees for implementing them are

low, and some programs will usually provide ongoing training for all participants, including willing parents and volunteers.

The Cultural Component

Like the recreational component, the cultural component offers students
opportunities to develop important skills that are not usually taught in the
classroom, such as hobbies, knitting, swing, skating, learning to play musical
instruments, and strategic board games like chess and Go. Other life-enhanc-
ing skills that could be included in the cultural component include etiquette,
interviewing skills, dressing for success, conflict resolution, and respecting
elders. Organizations like Boy Scouts, Girl Scouts, 4-H, and Big Brothers Big
Sisters have developed programs in these areas that have been successful in
developing these social skills among all children. If afterschool programs are
interested in these issues, they should not feel a need to reinvent the wheel,
but rather adopt and incorporate some of these other programs into theirs.

Training the Service Providers

Cognitive researchers like Vygotsky (1978), Piaget (1952, 1964), and
Confrey (1991) discuss the substantial qualitative and quantitative changes
that children undergo during the formative years and the importance of
meaningful interactions with cognitively stimulating experiences. They discuss the importance of having a more capable other, such as a guide, mentor,
or tutor, to provide just enough stimulation at the right time, which will, in
turn, provide the children with curiosity to learn. Piaget discusses the nature
of curiosity about how things work in his discussion of primary, secondary,
and tertiary circular responses. In his descriptions of children as "young phi-
losophers," Piaget, for example, reveals that the more complex situations
children are exposed to, the more likely they are to attempt to problem solve
by applying complex, logical problem-solving strategies. He discusses ac-
commodation and assimilation as crucial stages that children encounter
while challenging their knowledge of concepts. But, assimilation and accom-
modation cannot take place without the environment being set up in such a
way that the child will encounter objects, incidents, and conversations in the
environment that will challenge this knowledge.

Vygotsky (1978) also discusses this, but he does so from a different angle.
Although not ignoring the importance of what takes place in the mind of the
child, Vygotsky discusses the importance having a more capable other who is
able to guide younger children or less capable people to their best level of
capacity for learning, using the Zone of Proximal Development (ZPD). The
theory behind Vygotsky's arguments is that even if the environment is set up
to create stimulating situations for the children, if they are not exposed to a
more capable other who is able to scaffold for them in a way that will stimulate curiosity in the forms of dialogue and questions, then the amount of

growth that the child will experience will be limited. Vygotsky (1978) distinguishes between the actual and the potential Zones of Proximal Development, by defining the actual ZPD as the level at which the child is currently functioning. He describes the potential ZPD as the level at which the child could possibly function if provided with the correct type of stimulation and experience. However, the extent to which the children can reach their potential ZPD depends on the level at which the more capable other is currently functioning.

Although Piaget (1952, 1964) and Vygotsky (1978) discuss cognitive development from different perspectives, they both address an important and critical issue: the necessity and relevance of external stimulation via cognitively stimulating experiences. They both talk about the necessity of the child being in a cognitively stimulating environment to improve and enhance current and future cognitive functioning. The quality of the interaction that the child has with the stimulating environment and the more capable other depends on two things. First, they depend on the extent to which the adult has adequate knowledge of child development and cognition. Second, they depend on the extent to which the adult has the knowledge through training or otherwise, on how to scaffold, to mentor, and to communicate with the child, and this directly addresses the issue of training the staff. If the staff members are not trained to work with the students, then the programs should not expect to achieve the intended results, even if the proposal is well written, and the evaluation design and infrastructure are sound. The quality and training of the service providers are critical factors that also directly influence afterschool programs.

Regardless of the goals of the afterschool program, if the staff members are not properly trained to implement the program well, it is doomed to failure. Training includes teaching staff members how to work with children, how to negotiate, how to adapt to the needs of children of different ages, and how to implement the program's academic, cultural, and recreational components. Effective supervision is critical. As a part of the training, programs could include interim formative and summative measures that could serve as implementation checks to make sure that the staff members are performing their duties comfortably and correctly. Staff members should engage in frequent staff meetings and should also provide members with opportunities to present and solve problems that occur in the afterschool programs, such as discipline, academic, and other social problems. Staff members should be trained to recruit and supervise productive and proactive volunteers. This makes the difference between programs that retain volunteers and those that do not. If volunteers and staff members do not receive adequate training, well-intended adults who want to spend quality time with children may become frustrated, which, in turn, may lead to a high attrition rate. Some programs, such as AmeriCorps, VISTA, and the New York City Beacons have well-organized procedures to train their staff effectively, but many other programs do not have this capacity.

Specifically pertaining to academics, academically oriented afterschool programs should all have teaching-staff members with credentials, who practice teaching in the target areas, working with the children. Although volunteers may be instructors, an accredited instructor must be in a supervisory role, constantly overseeing and supervising the academic implementation of the programs.

In addition to the general training, it is also helpful if programs have implementation training and procedural manuals that must be used by the service deliverers. The training should include a specific number of professional or paraprofessional hours at the beginning stages of the program and continuous assessment toward these goals as the program progresses. Teachers, instructors, and volunteers who do not complete the training program should not work with the students.

Some afterschool and extended-school-day programs exist not only to provide additional, quality, educational instruction but also to improve community life between 3 p.m. and 6 p.m. Programs that focus on improving the lives of the students and their families have two responsibilities to fill. Their first responsibility is to provide a well-functioning haven for the children and their families who are being served. Their second responsibility is to find qualified, well-trained, caring staff members to work with the students to implement a positive afterschool program. Some examples of programs that have been able to do this are the New York City Beacons, LA's BEST, and the Baltimore Child First Authority. In addition to serving the children, these programs strive to involve the family and the community. Such programs encourage family and communities to volunteer and play active roles.

Research in the field of school reform shows that factors that contribute to academic achievement include using trained professionals in the programs and using methods of teaching that have been proven to work beyond the original sites (Fashola & Slavin 1998b; Slavin & Fashola, 1998). Some programs may not intend to train parents and community members to become instructional assistants or tutors because they do not intend to use them in this capacity. This does not mean that we should eliminate funding for programs that do not hire qualified teachers for afterschool or extended-school-day programs, but neither does it mean that we should keep untrained personnel in afterschool programs. Instead, personnel working in afterschool programs should be given the training they need to become effective in their roles. In some case, if the purpose of the program is to include volunteers, parents, and community and church members in low-income communities, one might expect to receive quite a few untrained personnel as volunteers, like the New York City Beacons and LA's BEST programs. However, it is possible to train the community volunteers, while including school personnel. The extent to which the volunteers receive training will depend largely on the goals of the programs, and the extent to which they plan to make a difference in the lives of the children.

Training Volunteers

As the afterschool program grows and becomes more widely known, programs will begin to involve community members as volunteers. Some programs make parental and community involvement mandatory. Whether their participation is mandatory or not, it is important to make volunteers feel welcome and useful. If the program is well structured, it should be easy to know the areas in which volunteer help will be needed and appreciated. A general orientation, followed by more specific training, will be helpful in welcoming and clarifying the role of the volunteer. The general orientation should introduce the community volunteers to the features of the program, including rules and regulations, interacting with students, mentoring, and identifying actions and characteristics that might eliminate students from the program.

If volunteers are expected to be involved in the academic components of the afterschool program, it is essential to train them as effective tutors. Create channels of communication that will facilitate a relationship between what is taught during the day and afterschool. In training volunteer tutors, it is important to address the attrition problem. Receiving time commitments for specific hours by volunteers will improve their effectiveness and overall quality.

Training Administrators

Without a sound administrative unit to organize its structural components and ensure that it runs smoothly and correctly, a program's effectiveness will be undermined. Although a school may opt to employ a program administrator who is not connected with the school, it may be preferable to hire someone familiar with the school. If the main goal of the program is academic, it is important for the administrator to maintain curriculum alignment. Other administrative responsibilities include checking qualifications of staff members and volunteers, organizing orientation for all participants, maintaining facilities, and overseeing payroll and accounting.

Other Considerations

Include Families and Children in the Planning

Especially in programs that offer cultural and recreational programs during the nonschool hours, families and the children themselves should be involved in the planning. If the activities to be offered are supposed to appeal to the interests of the children, they are certainly one of the best sources of knowledge about what will interest them. Generally, if the children and their parents are involved in the planning of the programs, they are more likely to stay involved.

Have an Advisory Board

Many school-based and community-based programs have an external board. LA's BEST, New York City Beacons, Child First Authority, and Murfreesboro Extended School Program are examples of programs that maintain strong links between community, families, religious organizations, and the school system. Such programs have boards made up of stakeholders who are responsible for the smooth running of the program and who make policy decisions about the programs also.

Another interesting and important aspect of afterschool research addresses the environmental elements of afterschool programs. Specifically, this aspect addresses the extent to which the afterschool atmosphere is conducive to the running of an effective afterschool program. Several studies that address this issue have been conducted, and although the various situations of the program have differed, the general outcome has been that students involved in the afterschool program have performed better when the atmosphere of the program was conducive to the goal of the program. Before drawing overwhelmingly general conclusions about the results of various studies, it is important to note that some aspects of climates might be conducive to the goals of some programs, but this is not always the case.

Pierce and colleagues (1997) studied the effects of program flexibility on outcomes for first graders in afterschool programs. There were two very different strands of findings in these results. The first strand examined the warmth of the staff members and the effect of this on the social developmental aspects of the students. The second strand of the results addressed the effects of program flexibility on the academic outcomes of the students.

These findings are important because they address two important questions: Should programs be flexible, and if so why? Depending on the goal of the outcome, flexibility may or may not benefit the program. If, for example, the goal of the program is to increase academic achievement in reading, asking the children to choose whether or not they will enroll in reading classes is not conducive to the goals of the program. Pierce and colleagues (1997) found that male students who had more flexible programs had significantly lower academic achievement scores in reading and mathematics. On the other hand, the social-emotional skills of the male students improved significantly if they were involved in the more flexible programs.

These findings imply that less-flexible academic afterschool programs might actually be more beneficial to students' academic achievement than flexible programs. Such an expectation is not really a far stretch of the imagination, especially if students involved in the study need academic assistance in certain curricular areas. Enrolling them in structured academic programs is one way to ensure that they attain the targeted academic goals. On the other hand, programs should be sure to afford children enrolled in cultural and recreational programs the flexibility to choose whatever programs they want to enroll in.

Other studies (Rosenthal & Vandell, 1996) have shown that children enjoyed supportive and flexible programs and rated the programs higher when the numbers of students enrolled in the programs were smaller. In some cases, afterschool programs have been known to have a negative effect on academic achievement on third-grade students (Vandell & Corasaniti, 1988). One main reason for this outcome was that students who attended the afterschool day care program were already stigmatized. Another reason was that the day care program was not developmentally appropriate for the third-grade students, and so students attending the program became bored and disruptive.

These are only a few results of studies of afterschool climates. They are included in this chapter because they are important factors to consider when creating afterschool programs. When all is said and done, if the climate in the afterschool program is not positive, students should not be expected to exhibit positive growth in the program.

Environmental Issues in Extended-School-Day and Afterschool Programs

Vandell and Corasaniti (1988), Posner and Vandell (1994), Rosenthal and Vandell (1996), and Pierce and colleagues (1997) have conducted evaluations on environmental issues of child care, key factors that contribute to the operation of effective afterschool programs, and the effects of different types of activities offered during afterschool programs. Some of these studies show links between academic success, and environmental issues and quality standards of care. This section presents some of the findings of these studies.

Climate and Flexibility in First-Grade Afterschool Programs

Pierce and colleagues (1997) studied experiences and subsequent academic and social-emotional adjustments of first-grade students enrolled in afterschool programs. They investigated the effects of program flexibility and staff members' warmness on first-grade students' academic, social, and emotional adjustments in school during the regular school day.

The study involved students in 38 school age child care (SACC) centers in and around Madison, Wisconsin. These centers offer various types of afterschool programs. Parents of the students were contacted by letter through their centers and then mailed a survey form. Of the 150 students in the study, 51% were male and 49% were female; 87% were Caucasian and 13% were minorities. Among the parents, 57% of the mothers and 67% of the fathers had obtained at least a bachelor's degree. Twenty-five percent of the children came from single-parent families.

This study assessed the climates of the programs, through classroom observation of the quality of the children's (positive or negative) interactions with one another as well as staff members' positive and negative regard, which included the frequency and quality of the staff members' interactions with the students. Program flexibility ratings were calculated based on the extent to which participants in the program were allowed to select their activities or playmates while involved in the afterschool program. Finally, the curricular activities were rated in terms of their number and age appropriateness.

Initial descriptive analyses found that such variables as socioeconomic status (SES), family structure, and firm or responsive parenting practices had a significant effect on the types of programs that students were enrolled in. Children who came from higher-income and two-parent-income families were more likely to be involved in programs offering greater flexibility and more activities and were also more likely to have better academic grades in mathematics, reading, and oral and written language. Children from single-parent and lower SES families, on the other hand, were more likely to be involved in programs in which staff members displayed more negative regard for children, and they were more likely to have poorer oral language grades. Firm or responsive parenting practices were associated with fewer negative peer interactions in the programs and better school adjustment, such as fewer externalizing behaviors, better work habits, better written-language grades, and better social skills with peers. SES and parenting practices were statistically controlled when examining these associations.

Boys involved in afterschool programs had significantly fewer internalizing ($p < .05$) and externalizing problems ($p < .01$) during the day if they experienced more, rather than less, positive regard from staff members. Negative staff member regard was associated with negative academic impacts, resulting in significantly lower reading ($p < .01$) and mathematics ($p < .05$) grades. Negative peer interactions also had an effect on adjustment. The more negative peer interactions the boys experienced during the afterschool program, the more internalizing ($p < .01$) and externalizing ($p < .01$) problems they exhibited and the poorer their social skills ($p < .05$). For girls, negative peer interactions were associated with externalizing behavior problems.

Social skills of the children improved significantly ($p < .05$) when they were involved in more flexible programs, but these students also had poorer written-language grades ($p < .05$) than students involved in less flexible programs. Looking at activities offered reveals that the more available and the greater the number of activities offered to the children, the better they were at solving both internal and external problems.

Finally, availability of activities offered showed the greatest impact of all the experiences for boys. Offering a wide array of available activities increased boys' internalizing problems ($p < .01$) and externalizing behaviors ($p < .05$), and decreased reading grades ($p < .01$) and math grades, ($p < .01$). For the girls, offering a wide array of activities did not have any relationship with the measured outcomes.

Because of its correlational nature, the Pierce and colleagues (1997) study cannot conclusively demonstrate that certain features of afterschool programs cause the various outcomes reported. However, this study does indicate that students are more likely to succeed in programs that offer more structure through fewer activities. It suggests that even for younger children, a well-structured program can have positive effects on the child during the nonschool hours as well as during the regular school day.

Atmosphere, Program Flexibility, and Academic Success in Afterschool Programs

Rosenthal and Vandell (1996) explored relationships between alterable features of SACC programs and older children's observed and reported experiences and parents' perspectives. These features included program structural variables, staff members' characteristics, and curriculum.

This survey involved 30 programs and 265 students in Wisconsin. The participants included a total of 170 children (94 in the third grade, 55 in the fourth grade, and 21 in the fifth grade). There were 103 males and 77 females, and the ethnic breakdown was 90% Caucasian and 10% minority.

Each site was observed twice. Children's interview reports on their experiences in the program were received ahead of time, and parent interviews were provided 2 weeks after the program observations. Results showed that classes with more staff members per child had fewer negative interactions between staff members and children and less negative child behavior. The lower the percentage of older children, the less negative behavior was found. More positive or neutral interactions with the staff members were observed when there was a greater flexibility of activities.

Children who were interviewed were asked to rate the programs based on overall climate, emotional support, and autonomy or privacy. A negative correlation was found between overall climate and total enrollment number; the more students enrolled, the lower the scores for climate. In addition, children in the larger programs rated them lower on perceived emotional support and autonomy, although these programs did offer a greater number of different activities. Finally, low staff-member-to-child ratios were also associated with negative parental ratings of the programs.

Academically Based Afterschool Programs and Third-Grade Achievement

Vandell and Corasaniti (1988) sought to investigate how afterschool care affected third-grade students' social, academic, and emotional development. First, they compared the responses of third-grade latchkey children to those of children who were in adult care during the nonschool hours. Second, they looked at the diversity of afterschool arrangements (day care centers, community sponsored sites, or at home with mother) and their effects on the social, emotional, and academic well-being of the students. Third, the researchers studied how different types of afterschool care were related to family structure (single, married, or divorced).

The subjects in the study were 150 Caucasian third graders in a suburb of Dallas. Most of the parents involved in the study were high school graduates and some had college experience. A preliminary descriptive analysis of the study showed that children whose fathers' educational levels were highest tended to stay with sitters afterschool instead of attending after-care centers or returning home alone (or to siblings). Outcomes evaluated in this study included academic grades, conduct grades, standardized-test scores—California Test of Basic Skills (CTBS), Iowa Test of Basic Skills (ITBS), College Ability Test (CAT), and The Association of Boarding Schools (TABS) test—classroom sociometric ratings (friendships with peers), teacher ratings (work skills), peer relations, emotional well-being, adult and child relations, parental ratings, and self-ratings.

Results of the study showed that the type of afterschool care had an effect on the sociometric ratings the students received from their peers. Children who attended the centers and those who went to a sitter after school were more likely to receive negative ratings from their peers than were students who returned home to their mothers or were latchkey children ($p < .01$).

The type of afterschool care also affected academic achievement. Specifically, children enrolled in centers had significantly lower ITBS scores than those who returned home to their parents. They also had significantly lower mathematics scores on the TABS and the CAT than did students in all other child care arrangements. Meanwhile, there were no significant standardized-test score differences between children in latchkey care and those who returned home to their mothers.

The socioemotional well-being of the students was also related to type of placement. Students who went to a sitter tended to have better senses of self-perception than did latchkey or center children. Finally, parents of children who attended centers rated their children as having lower peer relational skills than did parents whose children were in other forms of child care.

Descriptive data indicated that many of the students were stigmatized because they went to the center for afterschool activities. In addition to this, students who went to the centers were found to be already exhibiting behavioral problems. Furthermore, the activities in the centers were also rated as not being age appropriate. They were geared more toward children in lower grades, and thus the third-grade students in this study were bored.

Structured, Academic, Afterschool Programs and Low-Income Children

Posner and Vandell (1994) investigated the benefits of afterschool programs for low-income children. Subjects included low-income, minority (mostly African American), third-grade students in one of four types of afterschool care situations: maternal care, informal adult supervision, self-care, and formal afterschool programs. Almost 60% of the students qualified for free and reduced lunches, 50% were from single-parent families, and none of the parents had completed college.

Three afterschool programs were studied. One was housed at school but was primarily staffed by child care providers not classroom teachers. It provided a balance of academic, recreational, remedial, and cultural activities. The second had more of an academic focus and was staffed by teachers from the children's school-day programs. It focused on academic redemption and enrichment activities but also provided the children with cultural and recreational activities. The third program involved mainly recreational and cultural activities, with some homework assistance. All the schools had the same curriculum for the children during the day.

Outcomes measured included ratings of the children's behavior by the parents and the children, academic ratings of the children's success, report card grades, and standardized-test scores.

Preliminary descriptive analyses showed that African American children (who made up the majority of the population) were more likely to use adult supervision than self-care. Lower-income families were more likely than middle-class families to enroll their children in center-type, formal, afterschool programs, and children were more likely to return home to their mothers if their mothers were not employed.

Controlling for mother's education, child's race, and family income, students who attended afterschool formal programs performed better academically in mathematics, reading, and other subjects ($p < .01$), and had better conduct ratings than did children who were either in mother care or in other informal arrangements.

Children in all three formal school programs were rated as having better work habits than children who were informally supervised, and they were rated as being better emotionally adjusted than were students who were informally supervised and who returned home to their mothers. They were also rated as having better peer relations than children who were informally supervised. Children who were in formal afterschool programs or who went home to their mothers were less likely to be rated as antisocial than were unsupervised or informally supervised children, and they were also less likely to be rated as headstrong.

Children involved in the formally structured programs spent significantly more time on academics and enrichment lessons and significantly less time watching television or engaging in unorganized activities outdoors. They also spent significantly more time with adults and doing activities with adults. They spent significantly less time with siblings and more time with peers.

7

Evaluation

Why Evaluation Is Important

Evaluation should be built into an afterschool program. There are many different reasons for evaluating any type of educational research program, including accountability for money being spent on the programs, informing and educating the public, influencing policy, academic interest in what works, and so forth. The next section of the chapter concentrates on three reasons as they pertain to the evaluation of afterschool programs: accountability, sharing results, and the influence of educational reform.

Accountability

Evaluation is a form of information exchange and communication among program implementers, program evaluators, funders, policymakers, and the public. When program implementers receive funding, they are expected to have an impartial evaluator conduct whatever research was agreed on in the initial proposal and to have this research reported. The program implementers, evaluators, funders, and policymakers are responsible to each other and the public to explain how the various dollars are being spent in terms of program creation and implementation as well as the results and effects that these programs had. Evaluation is one way that the programs are able to fulfill this responsibility.

Sharing Results

As the interest in evaluating afterschool programs is relatively new, it is important for programs to inform other programs about their results so that errors will not be duplicated. Programs should not really be competing against one another but rather, they should be communicating with one another to show what does and does not work. There are more children in need of afterschool programs than there are programs to satisfy this need, and so afterschool programs should realize that the more they are able to share positive results, the more likely afterschool programs will be to obtain funding to continue.

As the programs work toward their goals, they are expected to track their progress and report the results of this progress. These results, in turn, influence policy, administration, education, and research. Currently, very little available research shows policymakers the results of afterschool programs on academic progress (Fashola, 1998). When programs share their results with external stakeholders, such as Congress, researchers, and other interested parties, they provide valuable information about the design, effects, and affects of the program on specific planned outcomes. For example, programs are able to share the results of effective, academically based afterschool programs on reading (Morris, Shaw, & Perney, 1990; Muir, 1974; Reid, 1989), which will allow potential afterschool programs to explore using them. This also helps the funders and entities to which the programs are accountable to use the research to help other districts that might be in need of assistance or additional academic and educational resources during the nonschool hours.

Evaluation results shared by the programs inform not just the external stakeholders but also the programs themselves. In both cases, evaluation is the language that this information exchange takes place in. For example, results will inform the programs being evaluated, and these, in turn, can be used to eliminate or improve the weaker components of the program and to keep the stronger components. Thus the sharing of the results of an effective evaluation enables all stakeholders to design and implement the most effective afterschool program possible.

Educational Reform

Recently, foundations, school districts, and local governmental agencies have begun to explore the concept of afterschool programs as a part of the whole school reform movement. The whole school reform movement has been around for decades and is constantly investigating additional ways to improve the educational opportunities and achievement levels of school-age children. One area that the movement has not thoroughly investigated or researched is academically based afterschool programs.

Many funders are providing specifically dedicated funding that is expected to improve academic achievement among children by providing them with academic tutoring and homework help sessions. This book does not advocate making the afterschool hours a direct replica of the regular school day, but, at the same time, we advocate using some of the time to provide the students with increased, enriched opportunities to learn. Some states, such as New Jersey, Maryland, and California provided funding to the school districts to provide academically based afterschool programs, with the expectation that the schools will improve their academic performance (Mott Foundation, 1999). Very little research, however, shows that afterschool programs are effective in attaining this goal (Fashola, 1998, 1999). This lack of information is due to lack of effective evaluations, and this could lead to two negative outcomes.

First, there is the possibility that because there is little information out there, it is possible for programs that were not effectively evaluated to receive funding, and they won't actually produce the desired results. If the funders do not see the results desired, they are likely to cut the funding for afterschool programs. Another, even more dismal, possibility is that policymakers and others looking to cut funding will interpret this lack of data due to lack of effective evaluations as proof that academically based afterschool programs are actually not effective in helping the population that they aim to serve.

If programs receiving funding are evaluated properly, then they will have an opportunity to influence and educate the educational world about the importance of additional or extended learning opportunities beyond the school hours. The results of this research, if performed well, will truly revolutionize the concept of the school day as we know it and add insightful research information to the field of school reform. Recently, more programs have been engaging in evaluations using rigorous designs. However, evidence of the effects of these programs is not readily available, so it is still difficult to draw widespread conclusions on the effects of afterschool programs on academic achievement. The new interest in rigorous evaluation of afterschool programs, however, is promising, and policymakers and funders should not cut the funds due to lack of evidence of effectiveness.

Effective Evaluations

Schools today are, in effect, consumers when it comes to implementing programs that can be used to bring about positive changes for their students. They are spending valuable funds to bring about this change. How can schools be sure that they are investing in the best possible program for the students in their district? The answer lies in investing in a program that has undergone an effective evaluation—one that has demonstrated evidence of effectiveness and generalizability to the population that it serves. All programs receiving funding for implementation of services should be required to show evidence that some type of evaluation is being conducted or evidence of evaluation. Evaluation can take many different forms. However, evidence of evaluation differs from evidence of effectiveness. For example, a survey of the program or even anecdotal information could qualify as evidence of evaluation.

Evidence of Effectiveness

Evidence of effectiveness is obtained by initially creating a robust experimental design that will provide results that are clearly attributable to the effects of the treatment. For example, one step to eventually obtaining evidence of effectiveness is to randomly assign students to two groups or to match students to two groups based on critical baseline data. It also involves comparing the two groups before and after the treatment. Some matching variables would include gender, ethnicity, socioeconomic status, grades, achievement level, pretest scores using fair measures, and, in some cases, level of English proficiency. This helps address some critical factors that could eventually produce results that may or may not be generalizable to other groups.

Generalizability is very important in evaluation research and is addressed in more detail shortly. For example, a program could operate a book club and measure success by documenting the number of books read by children in the program and children not in the program. If students were not randomly assigned to the two groups, it would be very difficult to determine the generalizability of any measurable changes. This means that if the students in the reading program had done better than students not in the group, we cannot ascertain the reason for the differences. The students could have been better readers at the onset of the treatment and so might have been more predisposed to reading more books, regardless of the treatment.

To provide evidence of effectiveness in afterschool programs, evaluators should draw their comparisons between competing afterschool programs rather than comparing students in an afterschool program to those in no afterschool program. If this is done, then the results can be interpreted as a result of that specific afterschool program, rather than as a result of any intervention at all. When programs are unable to provide evidence of effectiveness, it becomes the consumer's responsibility to determine the extent to which they can expect to see positive gains as a result of the program.

Generalizability

Previously, we discussed generalizability from the standpoint of the evaluator and the researcher. This section discusses generalizability as it relates to the consumer. As newly funded, afterschool initiatives seek to take on new programs, one question that they should ask the creator of the program is about the extent to which their results are applicable to the specific circumstances and population of the current site. This topic plays a big part in determining if the evidence of effectiveness will extend to the population that is actually being served by the school.

For instance, a program might experience success when used among middle-class students enrolled in private and non-Title I schools whose standardized tests scores are well above the norm. The afterschool program may have had little or no experience with low-income, Title I students who may be at risk for failure. This would lead one to question the generalizability of the program. For instance, how certain are the program creators that the program will experience the same type of success among students in the Title I populations? How will they address the issue of availability of funds or lack thereof, and how will it affect implementation and, eventually, the evidence of effectiveness of the program? How would this affect the generalizability of the results? Schools attempting to adopt externally developed programs should ask future service providers about the generalizability of their results. Specifically, they should explore the extent to which these programs have been used and evaluated with their population of students. Expensive programs without evidence of effectiveness in the specific targeted population should be able to justify asking for large amounts of money from pilot sites. Based on information provided, schools should be able to decide whether or not they will adopt the program and whether it is worth possibly excluding some students due to the fact that these programs are expensive and, therefore, difficult to expose to all the students in the school. These are some factors that make schools apprehensive about program adoption.

So, in essence, a program with a robust experimental design will provide results that are clearly attributable to the effects of the treatment and are generalizable to a specific population. Such a program's results will not be intentionally or unintentionally misinterpreted. Rather, they will lead schools to become better informed when implementing programs that claim to have evidence of evaluation or effectiveness. They will help schools to decide whether the program and results being presented to them are even applicable to the populations that they serve.

Creating a Solid Evaluation Infrastructure

Conducting an effective evaluation requires accurate and consistent communication of considerable amounts of information. A key factor that determines the quality of this information exchange is the existence of a strong evaluation infrastructure to serve as a communication channel among the various forces participating. An evaluation infrastructure consists not only of the physical mechanisms that pertain to evaluation, such as forms, surveys, and the evaluator or the evaluation team but also of the whole communication mechanism that exists among the various stakeholders involved in the program. Included in the scope of an effective evaluation infrastructure is the extent to which all the stakeholders understand and are committed to the importance of evaluation, the designation of key point people to gather data on schedule, clear and constant communication among parties, and an effective working relationship between the program implementers and the evaluators. If a solid infrastructure is built into the program, this, in turn, creates an environment for a realistic procedure that will allow for conducting effective ensuing evaluations.

Commitment to the Importance of Evaluation

The extent to which all the parties understand and agree with the importance of evaluation determines the degree of their commitment to the evaluation. When programs are committed to performing a sound evaluation, they know that evaluation is important if they desire to accomplish the program goals. They know that evaluation is something that they must do to accurately measure progress toward their accomplishments. If they are able to do this, the information will help them present honest and clear results that will help them to become effective in the future. When groups are not committed to the evaluation, they believe that evaluation is something that they must do to appease others and to continue to receive money. This means that there are very few (if any) direct benefits to the goals or implementation of the program. Noncommitted groups engage in program evaluation expecting to receive only good results and to hear only good things talked about.

The importance of the degree of commitment to the effectiveness of the evaluation infrastructure cannot be understated. It determines the extent to which the data-gathering aspect of the evaluation is functional and effective. If the infrastructure is strong, then it should function to fulfill the needs of all the parties involved. So, how do we make the infrastructure functional? The most important step is to include the stakeholders in the evaluation design. The evaluator, teachers, administrators, families, community members, and any other clusters of active participants must routinely meet and discuss the importance of evaluation, the needs of the evaluation group, what data are critical, and how these data should be gathered.

When the stakeholders are invited to participate in, and are actively included in, the planning of the evaluation process, they feel a sense of ownership and are more likely to be interested in participating. When forms are sent home for the parents to complete, they are more likely to do so if they have been a part of the process. Similarly, if community members are actively included as a part of the planning process, then they are more likely to complete and return surveys or other evaluation tools that they are given to fill out. Including the external stakeholders also involves educating them about the importance of evaluation as it relates to each of them specifically. For example, if they are included in the initial needs assessment planning meetings, then they will understand that the completion of the survey is directly connected to whatever resources are eventually made available by the funders.

Sometimes, it is helpful to include the parties in the actual designing of some of the evaluation tools before they are finalized, but this approach is more helpful with smaller-scaled and more-localized programs. If programs operate on a larger scale, it is more useful and effective to conduct evaluation workshops with the various parties early in the program in which the evaluation tools are designed.

Designation of Key Point
People to Gather Data on Schedule

As a part of the ongoing evaluation process, the programs should be expected to delegate a key person at each program, who is responsible for tracking the filling out of forms on a daily basis. They should identify and select key people to attend the workshops in which the tools are designed, who will then return to the schools and train their peers to use the data collection tools. This person should ensure that all the forms are complete and have been circulated among all the appropriate staff members and that the proper method of completion is understood by all the staff members responsible for filling them out. These people are responsible for making sure that enough forms are on hand all the time and that they are turned in regularly. To ensure that they are, indeed, turned in regularly, the data collection monitor should select a date (in collaboration with the staff members) when the form should be turned in. This date should be highlighted on the forms so that the staff members completing the forms will be reminded. This process will help to familiarize the various schools and programs with the evaluation process overall and also with the specific tools being used.

For example, in some afterschool programs, taking attendance at the beginning of each class can be a tedious process, and some teachers might choose to do it at the end of the day rather than when the students are present. An evaluation contact person at the school could assign specific teachers or volunteers to a program, whose main responsibilities are to go from class to class, gathering attendance information. This will facilitate the data-gathering process, and help the evaluator to create a more functional infrastructure.

Clear and Consistent Communication
Among the Evaluators, Program Implementers, and Stakeholders

Evaluation involves not only looking at the outcomes or impact of a program but also documenting the process and progress of the program. These two aspects of evaluation are actually referred to respectively as summative and formative evaluations and will be discussed in more detail in the section on types of evaluation. Regardless of the type of evaluations being conducted, it is important that all stakeholders remain in constant communication. The implementers and funders must always remain aware of one another's roles and expectations and keep the channels of communication open throughout the progress of the program. As the evaluator conducts both the formative and summative evaluations, input from the funders and implementers should shape the questions asked and the answers provided in the evaluation. Data forms and tools used must reflect the program being implemented and the expectations of the funders and link the two. If there are any concerns about the goals, components, or expected outcomes of the program on the part of the parties involved, the evaluators should be informed as soon as these concerns arise. The evaluator should be used as the link between the implementers of the program and the funding bodies, as it is the job of the evaluator to communicate what the programs are doing, why they are implementing the specific programs, and the extent to which the programs being implemented are working.

Working With Evaluators

There are many factors and variables to consider when working with evaluators. This section focuses on four specific factors that are likely to influence the relationships between the evaluator and the stakeholders: inclusion, communication, potential problem areas, and documentation.

Inclusion. Just as program development is an evolving process, so is program evaluation. Including the evaluator from the beginning helps funders, grantees, evaluators, practitioners, and administrators to have a better picture of the goals that they are trying to accomplish. Inclusion from the beginning also familiarizes the evaluator with all aspects of the program, thus helping everyone to emphasize strengths and eliminate weaknesses. When evaluators are included from the beginning, they become familiar with the program's goals and design long before the program has been implemented. Including evaluators from the beginning helps to avoid possible mistakes about the goals of the program, because they are able to provide advice from the beginning on what to do about the program, based on some prior knowledge. An evaluator who is not involved in the program from the beginning does not know enough about the key players in the program and cannot be seen as a source of information about the program. Not including the program evaluator from the beginning communicates the message that the evaluator is not pertinent to the program at all. This communicates the message that the evaluator is an outsider. Although this person may be able to provide some guidance to the staff members running the program, the information will not be pertinent to the growth and improvement of the program.

If the evaluator is included in the program early, it is still very important that clear and consistent communication channels be established among the programs, evaluators, funding agencies, and administrators—which is beneficial to all parties involved. Establishing clear and consistent communication helps all parties remain accountable to the terms of the program. This forms the beginning of a smooth evaluation process.

Communication. Establishing clear communication from the beginning helps to jointly establish goals, dates, and deadlines for evaluation of the program. This helps all the parties involved establish what outcomes they desire to bring about while there is still time to incorporate their ideas. When communication is established early, all the entities involved are able to come together and determine the feasibility of attaining these results and following the guidelines. Rather than seeing the evaluator as an outsider, establishing clear communication creates a feeling of collectiveness among all the parties, and the evaluation is perceived as owned by all the parties involved and, therefore, beneficial to all the parties involved.

When clear communication is not established early enough in the program's history, the evaluation process takes a different turn. For example, the evaluator alone sets the goals and objectives of the program as well as the deadlines of the evaluation, such as submitting the evaluation forms and setting assessment meeting times and dates. If the evaluator is not included from the beginning, these deadlines are difficult, if not impossible, to meet by the teachers and program deliverers. Not including the evaluator from the beginning means that the documentation needs of the program and the documentation needs of the evaluator are not the same. Evaluators may feel that they must create forms from scratch, but the program may have already created its own forms. Aligning the documentation among the various parties becomes difficult, if not impossible, and this creates unnecessary confusion and frustration for all parties.

It is quite possible that many of the programs may have established their own deadlines for turning in their own assessments and evaluations that they may have created, using their own forms. The feeling of having to duplicate the information will make the teachers feel overworked and not willing to do it. Including the evaluators from the beginning helps all the parties establish the deadlines, data collection, and outcomes desired and also helps use the feedback to inform all the parties involved. However, even if clear communication is established, all groups must realize that if they do not address the potential problem areas of the evaluation and assessment, they will experience very limited growth.

Potential Problem Areas. Even when programs choose to involve the evaluator from the beginning and show commitment and have good communication, some controversial issues always must be dealt with. Evaluations are difficult to perform even when everyone is committed. With this in mind, it is possible to avoid certain problematic issues before they begin. Discussing these areas ahead of time will make them less problematic. Not discussing them does influence your evaluation plan and makes the evaluation much less effective.

Some issues include developing the evaluation plan, having everyone agree on what the goals are, sticking to these goals, and holding everyone accountable to them. Negotiating a budget with an evaluator can also be seen as a possibly problematic area. If the budget is discussed ahead of time, it no longer becomes a hindrance. When potentially problematic issues are not discussed ahead of time, it is very likely that the evaluation plan, evaluation timeline, and budget will continuously have to be revised.

Documentation. One of the most important components and aspects of evaluation is documentation. Regardless of the type of evaluation being performed, it is important to remember that all documented information is important information. Therefore programs are encouraged to document all relevant information. Before doing this, all the parties must be informed of the necessary forms, surveys, interviews, and other types of information needed. All the parties must be educated about the importance and understand the relevance of the documentation to their programs. This works toward rapid acquisition of the data in the future.

Informed evaluators make their requests for documentation known early and inform their programs about the specific types of documentation needed. They explain how to complete the forms, and, in many cases, they provide the forms. Informed evaluators make sure that all schools keep uniform records and all the parties involved understand the terminology used in the records. This makes the collection and acquisition of data much easier.

On the other hand, if programs are not committed to the importance of documentation, the program implementers and the evaluators will experience frustration. If documentation is not taken seriously and requests for documentation are not made in advance, programs must resort to scrambling for information at the last minute. The information presented to the evaluators is usually not the type of information that the evaluator needs or wants. Another downfall is that the information that is eventually documented is not usually kept by all the schools and is not uniform across all the sites. Without relevant and correctly gathered data and documentation, evaluation is an impossible task.

When information is documented correctly and accurately, it provides all the parties with the information that is relevant to them as researchers. Program implementers are able to explore how they can improve the program; evaluators are able to investigate what works in the program, why it works, and recommend how to continue to make it successful. Funders, legislators, and other government officials are able to discover the impact and effects of their funding on the population.

Different Types of Evaluation

Setting up the evaluation infrastructure is important and is critical for the dissemination of the evaluation tools and data. An equally critical part of the infrastructure is determining the type of evaluation to be conducted. The groups collaboratively decide whether they wish to measure the descriptive components of the program, the impact of the program, or a combination of the two. The outcome of this collaboration will determine the type of evaluation to be conducted. Different types of evaluation include formative and summative, qualitative and quantitative, and ongoing and final evaluations. Although we mention six types of evaluations in this book, we mainly discuss formative and summative evaluations, with the understanding that qualitative methodology is used to conduct formative evaluations and quantitative methods are used to conduct summative evaluations. We also understand that all evaluations should be ongoing and that the results of the ongoing evaluations eventually feed the final evaluation. The stronger the ongoing evaluation, the better the final evaluation. We now proceed to describe, in more detail, formative and summative evaluations.

The first part of this section addresses the formative evaluation and how to use documentation and assessment to attain this information.

1) formative - Summative
2) Qualitative - Quantitaive
3) ongoing - final evaluation

Formative Evaluation Information

When initially establishing the program, it is important to document the steps taken. This type of information is usually useful for formative evaluations. Formative evaluations are generally descriptive in nature, using qualitative research to present the information. They differ from summative evaluations in that the information presented, although it does not provide evidence of effectiveness or the impact of the program, provides an intimate picture of the program being funded. Formative evaluations are able to document successes, victories, lessons learned, and other facts that are helpful to the overall assessment of the program. For example, if schools are implementing a new program, they should gather formative data that would help them document the steps taken to create the program, individuals who initially signed up for the program, the reasons that children initially withdrew from the program (if they did), and the initial staff members who signed up to teach in the program. The evaluation should also be able to document the various classes taught and whether or not other afterschool programs were held in the school at the same time. The formative evaluation does not address issues of sampling or selection bias but should keep records of how children were selected into the program. This helps the program prepare for possible selection limitations in the summative evaluation.

For the formative evaluation, types of data differ from those for summative evaluations because the goals of formative evaluations involve gathering data that inform the readers about the components of the program. To do this, programs must be able to track the participation of the participants regularly.

One basic way of doing this is by collecting various forms of descriptive information about the overall program and at different points in time. Tracking this type of information is important for the accuracy of the documentation pertaining to demographics of the program, and this will eventually influence the analyses to be conducted. If there are no formative data information mechanisms in place, then it will become almost impossible to conduct formative or summative evaluations.

For example, a program should create background information forms for all participants. These background information forms must be filled out with precision and accuracy because they will serve as very important sources of demographic information for the formative and summative evaluation. All the participants enrolled in the program must be required to complete the form to have accurate documentation on all the participants. Inaccurate and incomplete documentation will lead to inaccurate and incomplete evaluation, which is clearly of no use to anyone. Background information forms are just one example of formative information gathering tools. Examples of additional tools include survey forms, forms to measure progress periodically, and interview and observation forms. This information helps educate readers about various components and aspects of the program that otherwise might not be captured by the formative evaluations.

Outcomes. Programs and schools should ensure that they are collecting pertinent information for their own programs and should try to ensure that they have access to similar formative information for the control sizes. For example, the background information should be gathered for the control schools, also, to create an infrastructure that will allow the evaluator to compare the two groups, eventually, when the summative evaluation is conducted. They should be careful to report stumbling blocks that could potentially influence the results of the final summative evaluation. For example, they should report staff and student attrition and turnover and reasons that they occurred. They should also report how and why students were selected for the program. If, at any point, the program changes its goals, this should be communicated in the report. The formative evaluation should also specifically explain the goals of the program and the mechanisms in place in the program that are designed to meet the goals. Even in the formative evaluation, programs should look for things that could be potential confounding factors. If, for example, a school implements an academically based afterschool program, the formative evaluation should also include an account of programs used during the school days and how they may or may not be closely aligned with the afterschool program.

Summative Evaluation Information

Once the program and its components have been established and are in the process of being implemented, the next step is to begin to look for evidence of the impact of the program on its recipients. This type of information is usually largely investigated by the summative evaluation. Summative evaluations are usually quantitative in nature, using statistical analyses to interpret their findings. They differ from formative evaluations in that, if done well, their results show all interested parties that the program was definitely effective or definitely ineffective.

Summative evaluations are able to take into account various confounding variables and the effects of these variables on the results of the program. For example, some schools may be implementing a new, regular school-day program at the same time that they are implementing a new afterschool program. If the program evaluation is designed well, then the evaluators should be able to separate the two programs and the results of their effects. Well-designed summative programs avoid combining such variables as much as possible. Well-designed summative evaluations also address the endemic problem of selection bias and how it may or may not influence the interpretation of results.

For the summative evaluation, the types of data to be gathered and examined are slightly different from those for formative evaluations, because the goals of summative evaluations involve gathering and examining data that will eventually assess program impact and effectiveness. Overall outcomes to measure include attendance, behavior, parental and community involvement, and academic growth. To do this, programs must be able to track the participation and progress of their participants.

One basic way of doing this is tracking the attendance of all the parties involved. Tracking type of information is necessary for record keeping, accountability, documentation, and, eventually, for analysis. If there are no summative data information mechanisms in place, then it will be difficult to generate necessary information. As an example, a program should create daily attendance forms for all participants. These attendance forms must be filled out every day with precision and accuracy. Holidays and days in which the students take field trips should be carefully marked on the forms so as to account for accurate average daily attendance. These forms must be uniform across the sites, and all the sites must also use them. If programs are attempting to measure parental and community involvement, then they should create, disseminate, and complete separate attendance forms for them also. Although attendance forms filled out on a daily basis are pertinent to evaluation, they are not enough to measure the entire impact of the program. Programs also need to use additional information in their summative evaluations, such as demographic information about the participants. This type of information helps establish baseline data and also helps establish the basis for comparison to matched or control groups.

If the evaluation infrastructure is solid, the information requested in the background information forms has been jointly agreed on as necessary by the evaluator and the program administrators. This, in turn, will make it easier to collect the data expediently because all the parties have agreed to the information that needs to be collected. All the information gathered must always be kept confidential by all the parties. Some information to be collected in the background information sheets may includes name, date of birth, age, socioeconomic status, behavioral level, academic report card grades, academic standardized-test score information, number of parents in the household, number of siblings in the home and in the program, ages of siblings, gender, how they found out about the program, and—if the students leave the program—why they withdrew.

Additional information that the sites may choose to gather includes information about who expresses interest, who attends regularly, who attends the program initially, who attends the program more regularly, the attrition rate of the program, what components of the program the students like most, who leaves and why, and whether the students progress toward the various goals set by the evaluation committee. Some behavioral changes to measure include attitudes of participants toward work and authority and, specifically, toward peers and authority; behavior in general; willingness to cooperate; willingness to attempt new things; andwillingness to learn.

Outcomes. Programs and schools should make sure that they are gathering pertinent information for their own programs, and they should also try to ensure that there is a data collection mechanism for comparison sites. The data-gathering aspects of the evaluation infrastructure should be in place not only for the school that is implementing the program but also for the comparison school. This means that the summative and formative evaluation forms and surveys should be made available not only to the students in the treatment group but also to those in the experimental group. They should be careful to report the limitations of their studies and not overemphasize their results. For example, some programs may be comparing students in a high-academic afterschool program to similar students who are not receiving any academic remediation or enhancement.

Evaluation Design

When the results are reported, evaluators must also be sure to report the results of the comparison group. The evaluators must note the limitations and present the results with caution as they are comparing an afterschool program to no afterschool program, as opposed to comparing one afterschool program to another.

Programs must also be sure to look for confounding factors that might influence evaluation outcomes. For example, some programs may have taken on a new afterschool program but also taken on a new school-day reform program. It would be difficult to distinguish the results of the afterschool program from those of the regular school-day programs because one cannot really tell which one is influencing what. For instance, how can children who voluntarily attend an academic remediation program be compared to those who attend an academic enrichment program? And how can these two populations be compared to children who chose not to attend either? Simply controlling for prior achievement, grades, socioeconomic status, or other factors does not account for the obvious differences in motivations between children who select themselves into or whose parents select them into various programs.

There are solutions to these methodological problems, but they have rarely been applied. The best solution to this problem is to take a list of children applying for a given program and then randomly assign them to the program or to a waiting-list control group. This assumes that the afterschool program cannot serve all applicants, which is generally the case. The fact of applying and meeting other admission requirements ensures that the waiting-list control group is equivalent in all important ways to the treatment group. Of all the programs reviewed in this report, only the Howard Street Tutoring Program (Morris, 1990), the Memphis Extended-Day Tutoring Program (Ross et al., 1996), and the Exemplary Center for Reading Instruction used random assignment of this kind.

A less conclusive variant of this approach is to compare students who signed up first to participate in an afterschool program with those who signed up later. Again, the waiting-list students can be assumed to be similar to those who participated. There may be differences between children who signed up early and those who signed up later, but this design is far better than one that does not take self-selection into account at all.

A third research strategy would be to compare all children in a school (or eligible grades) who had the opportunity to participate in an afterschool program to all children in a matched control school who did not have such an opportunity. This comparison is appropriate only if a very high proportion of eligible children participate, and it might understate the program's effects because some of the children assessed would be ones who did not participate in the afterschool program. However, this design would solve the problem of self-selection.

At this stage of research and development of afterschool programs for elementary and secondary students, we find that there are a number of promising models in existence, many of which have encouraging but methodologically flawed evidence of effectiveness. Among programs intended to increase academic achievement, those that provide greater structure, a stronger link to the school day curriculum, well-qualified and well-trained staff, and opportunities for one-to-one tutoring seem particularly promising, but these conclusions depend more on inferences from other research than on well-designed studies of the afterschool programs themselves. Programs of all types, whether academic, recreational, or cultural in focus, benefit from consistent structure, active community involvement, extensive training for staff and volunteers, and responsiveness to participants' needs and interests.

Best Type of Evaluation

Ongoing and final – evaluation

There is a myth that one type of research and evaluation is always better than another is. For instance, some programs may believe that quantitative evaluations are much stronger than qualitative evaluations or that summative evaluations contain more useful information than do formative evaluations. In actuality, all the evaluation types work together to answer different types of questions about the evaluation. Formative evaluation influences summative evaluation, qualitative information influences quantitative information, and ongoing evaluation influences the final evaluation. The key for programs intending to undergo an evaluation is to be involved in all types of evaluation. Two types of evaluations, summative and formative, should be ongoing. Although programs are advised to begin their formative evaluations in the beginning, this type of research should be ongoing so as to continue to inform the program. As different aspects of the program evolve, evaluators must document these changes accurately if they intend to continue to evaluate the program.

Evaluating afterschool programs in an effective manner provides information that helps educate policymakers, researchers, educators, educational consumers, and all the stakeholders involved in afterschool programming about the importance and necessity of evaluation, especially if we plan to allocate large amounts of funding to these programs. Providing funding for rigorous and well-designed afterschool programs will enable the research base of afterschool programs to catch up to enthusiasm. Within the last 2 years, more funders are paying attention to the importance of research and are allocating funds at federal, state, and local levels that will allow for the various programs to engage in solid evaluations of their afterschool programs.

The final results of these efforts, however, remain to be seen. Currently, the results are promising, but without solid designs in place, it is premature to conclude whether or not results obtained from evaluations are strictly due to the specific afterschool interventions employed at the various sites. Programs like LA's BEST, Boys and Girls Clubs of America, Child First Authority, Foundations, 21st Century Community Learning Centers, and many other state and locally funded afterschool programs are interested in, and engaging in, evaluation of afterschool programs.

The results of these evaluations, if conducted well, will teach investors in afterschool programs lessons that we can use to strengthen the field of theory, research, and practice in this area. Well-performed evaluations in the field of after school will help us learn what to do as well as what not to do, rather than repeat mistakes of the past. A good example of this is the Head Start evaluation: In his work on the story of Head Start, Zigler shared the effects of not conducting both summative and formative evaluations when the program was in its beginning stages (Zigler, Finn-Stevenson, & Linkins, 1992; Zigler & Muenchow, 1992; Zigler & Styfco, 1993; Zigler & Valentine, 1973). Since the Head Start lesson, many federally funded intervention programs have been careful to add evaluation components to their overall programs in an attempt not to repeat past mistakes.

Program evaluation yields results that are useful for all the parties involved. Results from evaluations help to monitor what takes place on a day-to-day basis, as well as how successful the program was. They provide information about what could or should be changed, how it should be changed, and why it should be changed. Results of evaluations are important information for the dissemination and communication of information regarding afterschool reform. This information is not only useful to individual programs but also to other entities, including researchers and policymakers. If an evaluation is done well, it can be seen as a historical instrument, letting researchers, administrators, practitioners, and policymakers know what transpired during that period.

8

Conclusions and Implications: What Works

Patterns of Success Among the Programs

Specific Goals

Looking at some of the programs discussed in this chapter, we see that there are trends that the few programs that have achieved success show. First, the programs that achieved success were adapted in response to a need that existed among students of this specific population. This is also addressed in the needs assessment. For example, the programs saw a certain need to improve academic achievement—and assessed the reason that this problem existed: limited opportunities to learn. With this goal in mind, they focused on creating possible solutions: academically oriented afterschool programs that would provide them with increased opportunities to learn, thus eliminating the original obstacles to academic success. The basic structures of these programs were created in response to experiences within the communities; adaptations or modifications were developed to best serve each community.

Professional Development and Training

Second, once the target programs were created, another factor that has ensured success and effectiveness has been the training of the staff. For the programs reviewed in this chapter, academic success is measured by improvement of the academic grades of the students, and academic programs are programs created specifically to improve education in specific fields, such as reading, math, writing, and language arts. Most of the academically oriented programs in this book have staff members with credentials, who practice teaching in the target areas. Although volunteers may be instructors, accredited instructors have served in supervisory roles with the goal of overseeing the academic implementation of the programs.

An additional key role for the accredited academic staff member is that this person is responsible for training the staff members who implement the academic work with the students. In some cases, the accredited staff member actually teaches the students. Regardless, many of the programs placed teachers with credentials specializing in the areas of improvement in charge of the academic components of the program.

Many of the programs mentioned have implementation training-and-procedural manuals that must be used by the service deliverers. The training includes a specific number of professional or paraprofessional hours at the beginning stages of the program and continuous assessment toward these goals as the program progresses. Teachers, instructors, and volunteers who do not complete the training program do not work with the students. These programs also have manuals that provide curriculum material contents to be used in the academic programs.

Evaluation

A third feature that the successful programs share is that they have all been evaluated for evidence of effectiveness using pre-post and experimental-control quasi-experimental designs. This feature establishes confidence in the programs' effectiveness for future communities who desire to implement them. When afterschool programs are developed and evaluated effectively using these features, educators, parents, and administrators should expect positive results.

Because afterschool programs are seldom mandated for all children in a school, and in light of some of the prevalent barriers to implementing successful afterschool programs, some uncontrolled factor always influences why some children attend these programs and some do not. Assuming that afterschool programs cannot serve all applicants, we see that effective selection methods include random sampling, matching the treatment and the control groups on important basic demographics, or possibly comparing students who sign up for the program first to those who sign up later. As random assignment is not always possible, the additional methods mentioned, using pre-post and experimental-control quasi-experimental designs, are also desirable for evaluation for evidence of effectiveness. The effective programs have been successful at implementing one of these research designs.

Barriers to Participation in Afterschool Programs

In some cases, even when programs may have all the components, they may still have problem addressing the target population. Some programs may find that professional development, creating clear goals for the program, and evaluation of the afterschool programs are not enough to ensure success and sustainability of specific afterschool programs, if they do not address certain barriers to participation, even when the program has been well developed. This section addresses some prevalent barriers to participation in afterschool programs.

Transportation

In a survey conducted (Fashola, 1998) in 200 public schools (Title I) across the country, teachers were asked to state the top obstacles or barriers to participation in afterschool programs. The schools reported that the most frequent obstacle was transportation. This suggests a strong relationship between the availability of transportation and the extent to which a program can successfully serve its target population. In this case, it is important to find creative ways to address this. Bussing alternatives are solutions adopted by some programs for their clientele (U.S. National Education Commission on Time and Learning, 1992), and others have created programs within the neighborhoods of the clientele that they serve (such as Child First Authority, 21st Century Community Learning Centers, New York City Beacons, and LA's BEST). But this is not enough to eliminate the transportation concern. For example, some of the children may be too young to walk home at the end of the day even if the program exists in the neighborhood. In other cases, for instance, during the winter months, parents may not wish to have their children walking home in the dark, and they may opt not to enroll their children in afterschool programs. In still other cases, students' transportation passes may expire prior to the end of the afterschool program, thus making it difficult for students to afford and use affordable transportation. In any case, it is important to find creative ways to address this.

Cost

Affordability is another real barrier to afterschool participation. Some good programs cost money, and this tends to be a big barrier to participation in the program for many families. Sometimes, students in the programs have siblings who could benefit from the programs, but providing these families with discounts in enrollment still will not necessarily facilitate access to the program. Afterschool service providers must be sure to research the communities of their targeted populations and explore ways to make the program more accessible and available to them. Some of the programs researched in this chapter have nominal or minimal costs attached to them.

The issue of cost also affects the staff. Usually, a good and qualified staff costs more money. The more academically specialized the program, the more the program should expect to pay the staff. The cost factor also indirectly influences the attendance of these students, because to pay the teachers appropriate salaries, programs may have to charge.

Siblings

This barrier to afterschool participation is also very real. Programs attempting to cater to older students would be more likely to experience this threat than would programs catering to younger children. In this case, many older students who do not have siblings enrolled in the program will eventually be lost because they are responsible for taking care of their younger siblings who are not enrolled in the program. The extent to which programs are able to serve siblings who are also in need of afterschool services will determine the extent to which the afterschool programs can serve their targeted populations.

There are undoubtedly many, many programs in existence in our communities that attempt to develop the talents of students during the nonschool hours, but there are also many barriers to these programs successfully achieving their goals. Among programs intended to increase academic achievement, those that provide greater structure, a stronger link to the school-day curriculum, well-qualified and well-trained staff, and opportunities for one-to-one tutoring seem particularly promising. Programs of all types, whether academic, recreational, or cultural in focus, appear to benefit from consistent structure, active community involvement, extensive training for staff and volunteers, and responsiveness to participants' needs and interests.

The programs reviewed in this book have, in some way, overcome these barriers and thus proven successful. This is not to say that these are the only programs that have ever benefited students during the afterschool hours. Rather, this book shows that the programs in existence could possibly look at some of the specific factors that have made these programs successful and implement them themselves. Perhaps one of the most salient factors among all the factors is that there are people in the communities and in the lives of the children who are dedicated to further enriching the lives of the children. However, barriers, such as lack of training, cost and affordability, transportation, and lack of evidence of effectiveness of the programs plague their ability to sustain themselves.

Conclusion

There is no straightforward answer to the question of what works best in afterschool programs. The answer depends on why the program was initially created, the extent to which the program design addresses the needs of the participants, and the extent to which the program shows positive outcomes when evaluated for evidence of effectiveness. If the program was created because of concerns about increasing amounts of crime and violence, then the program that works is one proven to alleviate this problem. If the program was set up to enhance academic gains, then the program that works is one proven to be effective for this purpose.

Programs reviewed in this book suggest that research on afterschool programs is at a very rudimentary stage. Few studies of the effects of afterschool programs on achievement or other outcomes meet minimal standards of research. Many of these studies suffer from selection bias. Because afterschool programs are seldom mandated for all children in a school, some uncontrolled factor always influences why some children attend these programs and some do not. Most often, afterschool programs are voluntary, so, presumably, it is more highly motivated children (or children of more motivated parents) who attend them. In other cases, afterschool programs are set up to be remedial or to serve at-risk children, so those who attend them are likely to be worse off (before attending the program) than those who do not. Comparisons of alternative afterschool programs have the same problem.

Initially, when this book was conceived, we found that a number of promising models existed, many of which had encouraging but also methodologically flawed evidence of effectiveness. Among programs intended to increase academic achievement, those that provided greater structure, a stronger link to the school day curriculum, well-qualified and well-trained staff, and opportunities for one-to-one tutoring seemed particularly promising, but these conclusions depended more on inferences from other research than from well-designed studies of the afterschool programs themselves. At this point, research on academically based afterschool programs was relatively new. Now, programs of all types—whether academic, recreational, or cultural in focus—appear to benefit from consistent structure, active community involvement, extensive training for staff and volunteers, and responsiveness to participants' needs and interests.

We need much more research on the effects of all types of afterschool programs, especially those intended to enhance student achievement. There is a particular need for development and evaluation of replicable, well-designed programs capable of being used across a wide range of circumstances.

This book has described a number of programs that are being used, or are capable of being used, during the nonschool hours. Readers should see these programs as interesting alternatives that offer practical ideas and some indications of how afterschool programs might be created, implemented, and evaluated. This book provides afterschool and extended-day program developers and directors, researchers, schools, and communities with the opportunity to examine different types of programs, to examine evidence of effects, and to build on or select the components or programs that best fit their needs when designing afterschool programs—and also to evaluate the programs and thereby make them sustainable and reliable.

It is not the intent of this book to replace regular school-day programs with afterschool programs but, rather, to use the afterschool hours to address the needs of children, schools, communities, and families and to understand their importance and take advantage of the positive outcomes that programs could show if implemented and evaluated properly. Afterschool programs are increasing rapidly and have received strong support from the Clinton administration, from Congress, and from state and local policymakers, and thus it is important to ensure that we create infrastructures that will make these programs sustainable beyond the lives of Senate and presidential terms.

Resources

Contacts for Information on Programs Reviewed

Big Brothers Big Sisters of America
230 North 13th Street
Philadelphia, PA 19107
(215) 567-7000
www.bbbsa.org

Book Buddies
Mary Ann Elwood, Volunteer Coordinator
1400 Melbourne Road
Charlottesville, VA 22901
(804) 984-7038
www.curry.edschool.virginia.edu/curry/dept/cise/read/bookbuds/

Curry School of Education, McGuffey Reading Center
Ruffner Hall, University of Virginia
405 Emmet Street
Charlottesville, VA 22903
(804) 924-3111

Marcia Invernizzi
1828 Yorktown Drive
Charlottesville, VA 22901

Books and Beyond
309 North Rios Avenue
Solana Beach, CA 92075
(858) 755-3823
Fax: (858) 755-0449
e-mail: booksbey@sbsd.sdcoe.k12.ca.us
www.booksandbeyond.org

Boys & Girls Clubs of America
1230 West Peachtree Street, N.W.
Atlanta, GA 30309
(404) 815-5700
e-mail: swilder@bgca.org
www.bgca.org

Boy Scouts of America, National Council
P.O. Box 152079
Irving, Texas 75015-2079
(800) 323-0732
www.bsa.scouting.org

Camp Fire Boys and Girls
Stewart J. Smith, Executive Director
4601 Madison Avenue
Kansas City, MO 64112-1278
(816) 756-1950
Fax: (816) 756-0258
e-mail: info@campfire.org
www.campfire.org/campfire_nf.html

Child First Authority (CFA)
Carol Reckling, Executive Director
3000 Druid Park Drive
2nd Floor, Suite A
Baltimore, MD 21215
(410) 367-8520
Fax: (410) 367-8523
e-mail: ChildFirst@juno.com

Coca-Cola Valued Youth Program
Josie D. Supik
Intercultural Development Research Association
5835 Callaghan Road, Suite 350
San Antonio, TX 78228
(210) 684-8180
Fax: (210) 684-5389

Early Identification Program
Robert Stark, Program Developer
(513) 483-6793
Barb Hutzel, Coordinator
(513) 554-1001

Reading School District
1301 Bonnell Avenue
Cincinnati, OH 45215

Exemplary Center for Reading Instruction (ECRI)
Ethna R. Reid, Reid Foundation
3310 South 2700 East
Salt Lake City, UT 84109
(801) 486-5083 or (801) 278-2334
Fax: (801) 485-0561

Explore Incorporated
Sarah Hoit, Founder
4900 Wetheredsville Road, Suite 1C
Baltimore, MD 21207
(888) 413-9756 or (410) 448-9930

Extended-Day Tutoring Program in Memphis City Schools
Stephen M. Ross, Associate Director and Senior Researcher
Center for Research in Educational Policy, Success For All Program
204 Browning Hall
University of Memphis
Memphis, TN 38152
(901) 678-3413
e-mail: smross@memphis.edu

Fifth Dimension
Michael Cole
Laboratory of Comparative Human Cognition
University of California, San Diego
9500 Gilman Drive
La Jolla, CA 92093-0092
(858) 534-4006
Fax: (858) 534-7746
http://lchc.ucsd.edu/Projects/5th.dim_desc.html

Foundations Inc.
Rhonda H. Lauer, Chief Executive Officer
100 Executive Drive, Suite 1
Moorestown, NJ 08057
(856) 727-8000
Fax: (856) 727-8815
www.foundations-inc.org

Girl Scouts of the U.S.A.
Elinor Johnstone Ferdon
Mary Rose Main
420 Fifth Avenue
New York, NY 10018-2798
(212) 852-8000
www.gsusa.org

Hands On Science Outreach (HOSO)
Benjamin Brandt, Executive Director
12118 Heritage Park Circle
Silver Spring, MD 20906
(301) 929-2330 or (888) HOSO-888
e-mail: hoso@radix.net
www.hands-on-science.org

Help One Student To Succeed (HOSTS)
William E. Gibbons
8000 N.E. Parkway Drive, Suite 201
Vancouver, WA 98662-6459
(206) 260-1995 or (800) 833-4678
Fax: (206) 260-1783

Howard Street Tutoring Program (HSTP)
Darrell Morris
Appalachian State University
Boone, NC 28608
(828) 262-2000

Imaginitis Learning System
George E. Simon, Vice President, Sales and Marketing
Lynne A. Cisney, Manager, Sales Services
Imaginitis Interactive, Inc.
435 Devon Park Drive, Suite 301
Wayne, PA 19087
(800) 610-2549

Increased Maximal Performance by Activating Critical Thinking (IMPACT)
S. Lee Winocur, National Director
Center for the Teaching of Thinking
21412 Magnolia Street
Huntington Beach, CA 92646
(714) 964-3106

Intergenerational Literacy Tutorial Program
Alison Dwyer
Boston Partners in Education
44 Farnsworth Street
Boston, MA 02210
(617) 451-6145, ext. 603
e-mail: adwyer@jsi.com
www.bostonpartners.org/initiatives/intergen.htm

Junior Great Books Curriculum (JGBC)
Great Books Foundation
35 East Wacker, Suite 2300
Chicago, IL 60601-2298
(800) 222-5870

LA's BEST
Carla Sanger, President and CEO
Corporate Office
Office of the Mayor
200 North Main Street, Suite 700
Los Angeles, CA 90012
(213) 847-3681
Fax: (213) 485-6606
e-mail: csanger@mayor.lacity.org

Operations Office
Los Angeles Unified School District
450 North Grand Avenue, P-103
Los Angeles, CA 90012
(213) 625-4024
Fax: (213) 626-5106
www.lasbest.org

Mindsurf
Mindsurf Networks
8180 Queensboro Drive, Suite 500
McLean, VA 22102
(703) 848-4420

Murfreesboro Extended School Program (ESP)
Marilyn M. Mathis, Director of Schools
Murfreesboro City Schools
2552 South Church Street
Murfreesboro, TN 37127

(615) 893-2313
Fax: (615) 893-2352

National Association of Police Athletic Leagues
618 U.S. Highway 1, Suite 201
North Palm Beach, FL 33408-4609
(561) 844-1823
Fax: (561) 863-6120
e-mail: copnkid1@aol.com
www.nationalpal.org

National 4-H Council
7100 Connecticut Avenue
Chevy Chase, MD 20815
(301) 961-2800
e-mail: info@fourhcouncil.edu
www.4-h.org
www.fourhcouncil.edu

New York City Beacons
Jennie Soler-McIntosh
Department of Youth and Community Development
156 Williams Street
New York, New York 10038
(212) 676-0453
Fax: (212) 442-4773

Peter Kleinbard
Fund for the City of New York
121 Sixth Avenue
New York, NY 10013-1505
(212) 925-6675
Fax: (212) 925-5675
www.nccic.org/ccpartnerships/profiles/beacons.htm

Project Success Enrichment
Carolyn Bronson, Project Director
Box 22447
Seattle, WA 98122-0447
(206) 325-5418

Reading Recovery
Carol A. Lyons
Gay Su Pinnell
Diane E. DeFord
Ohio State University

200 Ramseyer Hall
29 West Woodruff Avenue
Columbus, OH 43210
(614) 292-7807

Read Write Now!
U.S. Department of Education
(800) USA-LEARN
www.udel.edu/ETL/RWN/

Study Skills Across the Curriculum (SSAC)
Patricia S. Olson, Director
1897 Delaware Avenue
West St. Paul, MN 55118
(612) 681-0844 or (612) 898-3002
Fax: (612) 681-0879

Voyager Expanded Learning
1125 Longpoint Avenue
Dallas, TX 75247
(888) 399-1995 or (214) 631-0999
(888) 399-1995
www.voyagerlearning.com

References

Adler, M. (1982). *The Paideia proposal: An educational manifesto.* New York: MacMillan.

Baltimore Police Department Division of Planning and Research. (1998). *Juvenile victimizations comparison for Goodnow PAL center area.* Baltimore: Baltimore Police Athletic League.

Blanton, W., Moorman, G. B., Hayes, B. A., & Warner, M. L. (1996, April). *Effects of participation in the Fifth Dimension on far transfer* (Technical Report No. 3). Boone, NC: Appalachian State University, College of Education, Laboratory on Technology and Learning.

Blanton, W. E., Mayer, R. E., & Shustack, M. (1995). *Effects of participation in the Fifth Dimension on near and far transfer: A summary.* Boone, NC: Appalachian State University, College of Education, Laboratory on Technology and Learning.

Block, J. H., Everson, S. T., & Guskey, T. R. (1995). *School improvement programs.* New York: Scholastic.

Books and Beyond. (1983). *Proposal submitted to the Program Effectiveness Panel of the U.S. Department of Education.* Washington, DC: U.S. Department of Education.

Books and Beyond. (1995). *Proposal submitted to the Program Effectiveness Panel of the U.S. Department of Education.* Washington, DC: U.S. Department of Education.

Boyer, E. L. (1987). Early schooling and the nation's future. *Educational Leadership, 44*(6), 4-9.

Bronfenbrenner, U. (1986). Alienation and the four worlds of childhood. *Phi Delta Kappan, 67*(6), 430, 432-436.

Brooks, P. E., & Herman, J. L. (1991). *LA's BEST: An after-school education and enrichment program: Evaluation report.* Los Angeles: University of California, Center for the Study of Evaluation.

Brooks, P. E., Mojica, C. M., & Land, R. E. (1995). *Final evaluation report: Longitudinal study of LA's BEST after-school education and enrichment program, 1992-94.* Los Angeles: University of California, Center for the Study of Evaluation.

Bureau of Labor Statistics. (1997). *Annual average figures from the current population survey.* Washington, DC: Government Printing Office.

Burns, C., Jr. (1992). Meeting the academic needs of children after school. *NAASP Bulletin, 76,* 120-122.

Campbell, L. P., & Flaker, A. E. (1985). Latchkey children: What is the answer? *Clearing House, 58*(9), 381-383.

Canada, G. (1996). The Beacons: Building healthy communities. *Community Education Journal, 23*(3), 16-18.

Cardenas, J. A., Montecel, M. R., Supik, J. D., & Harris, R. J. (1992). The Coca-Cola Valued Youth Program: Dropout prevention strategies for at-risk students. *Texas Researcher, 3,* 111-130.

Carnegie Corporation of New York. (1989). *Turning points: Preparing American youth for the 21st century* (Report of the Task Force on Education of Youth Adolescents). New York: Author.

Carnegie Corporation of New York. (1992). *A matter of time: Risk and opportunity in the non-school hours* (Report of the Task Force on Youth Development and Community Programs). New York: Author.

Carnegie Corporation of New York. (1994). Starting points: Executive summary of the report of the Carnegie Corporation of New York Task Force on meeting the needs of young children. *Young Children, 49*(5), 58-61.

Carnegie Corporation of New York. (1995). *Great transitions: Preparing adolescents for a new century* (Concluding report of the council). New York: Author.

Carnegie Council on Adolescent Development. (1994). *Consultation on after-school programs.* New York: Carnegie Corporation of New York.

Clay, M. M. (1985). *The early detection of reading difficulties.* Exeter, NH: Heinemann.

Clinton, Bill. (1997). "State of the Union Address." Retrieved March 28, 2001, from the World Wide Web: www.law.ou.edu/hist/state97.html

Clinton, Bill. (1998). "State of the Union Address." Retrieved March 28, 2001, from the World Wide Web: www.washingtonpost.com/wp-srv/politics/special/states/docs/sou98.htm

Clinton, Bill. (1999). "State of the Union Address." Retrieved March 28, 2001, from the World Wide Web: www.washingtonpost.com/wp-srv/politics/special/states/docs/sou99.htm

Clinton, Bill. (2000). "State of the Union Address." Retrieved March 28, 2001, from the World Wide Web: www.abcnews.go.com/sections/us/DailyNews/clintonspeech1.html

Coca-Cola Valued Youth Program. (1991). *Proposal submitted to the Program Effectiveness Panel of the U.S. Department of Education.* Washington, DC: Government Printing Office.

Cole, M. (1994a). *First year report: July 1994-June 1995: Using new information technologies in the creation of sustainable after-school literacy activities: From invention to maximizing potential* (Andrew W. Mellon Foundation research proposal, UCSD 94-7098). La Jolla: University of California, San Diego, Laboratory of Comparative Human Cognition.

Cole, M. (1994b). *Using new information technologies in the creation of sustainable after-school literacy activities: From invention to maximizing potential* (Andrew W. Mellon Foundation research proposal, UCSD 94-7098). La Jolla: University of California, San Diego, Laboratory of Comparative Human Cognition.

Confrey, J. (1991). Steering a course between Vygotsky and Piaget. *Educational Researcher, 20*(8), 28-32.

Council of Chief State School Officers. (1987). *Characteristics of at-risk students.* Washington, DC: Author.

Criscuola, M. M. (1994). Read, discuss, reread: Insights from the Junior Great Books Program. *Educational Leadership, 51*(5), 58-61.

DeFord, D. E., Pinnell, G. S., Lyons, C., & Young, P. (1988). *Reading recovery: Volume IX: Report on the follow-up studies.* Columbus: Ohio State University.

de Kanter, A., Pederson, J., & Bobo, L. M. (1997). *Keeping schools open as community learning centers: Extending learning in a safe, drug-free environment before and after school.* Washington, DC: U.S. Department of Education.

Engman, R. (1992). On a roll: A successful after-school tutoring program at Patrick Henry School, Alexandria, Virginia. *Principal, 71*(3), 24-25.

Fashola, O. S. (1998). *Review of extended-day and after-school programs and their effectiveness* (Report No. 24). Baltimore: Johns Hopkins University, Center for Research on the Education of Students Placed at Risk.

Fashola, O. S. (1998). *What Title I schools have to say about their after-school programs.* Paper presented at the annual meeting of the American Educational Research Association, San Diego, CA.

Fashola, O. S. (1999). *The Child First Authority after-school program: A descriptive evaluation* (Report No. 38). Baltimore: Johns Hopkins University, Center for Research on the Education of Students Placed at Risk.

Fashola, O. S. (in press). *Child First Authority: Third year report, executive summary.* Baltimore: Johns Hopkins University Press, Center for Research on the Education of Students Placed at Risk.

Fashola, O. S., & Slavin, R. E. (1997). Promising programs for elementary and middle schools: Evidence of effectiveness and replicability. *Journal of Education for Students Placed at Risk 2*(3), 251-307.

Fashola, O. S., & Slavin, R. E. (1998a). Effective dropout prevention and college attendance programs. *Journal of Education for Students Placed at Risk, 3*(2), 160-182.

Fashola, O. S., & Slavin, R. E. (1998b). Schoolwide reform programs: What works? *Phi Delta Kappan, 79*(5), 370-379.

Fleming-McCormick, T., & Tushnet, N. C. (1996, April). *Does an urban 4-H program make differences in the lives of children?* Paper presented at the annual meeting of the American Educational Research Association, New York City.

Freiertag J., & Chernoff, L. (1987). Inferential thinking and self-esteem: Through the Junior Great Books Program. *Childhood Education, 63*(4), 252-254.

Frymier, J., & Gansneder, B. (1989). The Phi Delta Kappa study of students at-risk. *Phi Delta Kappan, 71*, 142-146.

Furby, L., & Beyth-Marom, R. (1990). *Risk taking in adolescence: A decision-making perspective.* Washington, DC: Carnegie Council on Adolescent Development.

Galambos, N. L., & Maggs, J. L. (1991). Out-of-school care of young adolescents and self-reported behavior. *Developmental Psychology, 27*(4), 644-655.

Gallegos, G. (1995). *Investing in the future: HOSTS evaluation for the Pasadena Independent School District.* Vancouver, WA: Hosts Corp.

Goodman, I. F., & Rylander, K. (1993). *An evaluation of children's participation in the Hands On Science Outreach Program.* Cambridge, MA: Sierra Research Associates.

Grossman, J. B., & Garry, E. M. (1997). *Mentoring—a proven delinquency prevention strategy.* Washington, DC: U.S. Department of Justice, Office of Juvenile Justice and Delinquency Prevention.

Halpern, R. (1992). The role of after-school programs in the lives of inner-city children: A study of the Urban Youth Network. *Child Welfare, 71*(3), 215-230.

Hamilton, L. S., & Klein, S. P. (1998). *Achievement test score gains among participants in the foundations school age enrichment program.* Santa Monica, CA: RAND.

Hamilton, L. S., Le, V., & Klein, S. P. (1999). *Foundations school-age enrichment program: Evaluation of student achievement.* Santa Monica, CA: RAND.

Harris, A. J., & Jacobson, M. D. (1980). A comparison of the Fry, Spache, and Harris-Jacobson readability formulas for primary grades. *Reading Teacher, 33*(8), 920-924.

Henderson, D. (1990). Expanding the curriculum with after-school classes, Oak Park Valley Union Elementary School District, Tulare, California. *Thrust, 1,* 32-33.

HOSTS Corporation. (1994). *Independent evaluations of the HOSTS structured mentoring program in language arts.* Vancouver, WA: Author.

Huang, D., Gribbons, B., Kim, K. S., Lee, C., & Baker, E. L. (2000). *A decade of results: The impact of the LA's BEST after-school enrichment program on subsequent student achievement and performance.* Los Angeles: UCLA Graduate School of Education and Information Studies, Center for the Study of Evaluation.

Huck, C. S., & Pinnell, G. S. (1986). *The Reading Recovery Project in Columbus, Ohio: Pilot year, 1984-85.* Columbus: Ohio State University.

Invernizzi, M., Juel, C., & Rosemary, C. A. (1996). A community volunteer tutorial that works. *Reading Teacher, 50*(4), 304-311.

Jacoby, M. D. (1989). School improvement and after-school programs: Suggestions to deal with the "latchkey" children problem. *Journal of Educational Public Relations, 12*(2), 14-19.

Johnson, D.W., & Johnson, R.T. (1996). Teaching all students how to manage conflicts constructively: The peacemakers program. *Journal of Negro Education, 65*(3), 322-335.

Jones, J. H., (1994). Ahead of the times in Murfreesboro. *School Administrator, 51*(3), 16, 18-21.

Jones, J. H. (1995). Extending school hours: A capital idea. *Educational Leadership, 53*(3), 44-46.

Kuenzer, K. (1978). Junior Great Books: An interpretive reading program. *School Library Journal, 24*(9), 32-34.

Laboratory of Comparative Human Cognition. (1994). *How-to manual to La Clase Magica: A bilingual/bicultural Fifth Dimension site.* La Jolla: University of California, San Diego, Laboratory of Comparative Human Cognition.

Lakes, R. D. (1996). *Youth development and critical education: The promise of democratic action* (SUNY series: Democracy and Education). New York: State University of New York Press.

Marx, F. (1989). *After-school programs for low-income young adolescents: Overview and program profiles* (Working Paper No. 194). Wellesley, MA: Wellesley College, Center for Research on Women.

Marx, F. (1990). *School age child care in America: Final report of a National Provider Survey* (Working Paper No. 204). Wellesley, MA: Wellesley College, Center for Research on Women.

McAdoo, H. P., & Crawford, V. A. (1988). *Project SPIRIT evaluation report: 1987-1988.* Washington, DC: Congress of National Black Churches.

McGillis, D. (1996). *Beacons of hope: New York City's school-based community centers: Program focus.* Washington, DC: Department of Justice, National Institute of Justice.

Mercure, M. (1993). Project achievement: An after-school success story. *Principal, 73,* 48-50.

Milch, N. (1986). After-math: A program for after-school help. *NAASP Bulletin, 70*(1), 107-109.

Mitchell, J.M. (1996). *The impact of the Imaginitis Learning System on cooperation and conflict resolution, results of a three-year evaluation* (Preliminary report). Minneapolis: Cooperative Learning Center, University of Minnesota.

Morris, D. (1990). *The Howard Street Tutoring manual: Case studies in teaching beginning readers.* Boone, NC: Appalachian State University Reading Clinic.

Morris, S. W. (1992). *What adolescents want and need from out-of-school programs: A focus group report.* Bethesda, MD: Author.

Morris, D., Shaw, B., & Perney, J. (1990). Helping low readers in Grades 2 and 3: An after-school volunteer tutoring program. *Elementary School Journal, 912,* 132-150.

Morton-Young, T. (1995). *After-school and parent education programs for at-risk youth and their families: A guide to organizing and operating a community-based center for basic educational skills reinforcement, homework assistance, cultural enrichment, and a parent involvement focus.* Springfield, IL: Charles C Thomas.

Mott Foundation. (1999). *After-school alliance, after-school alert poll report: A report of findings from the J.C. Penney Nationwide Survey on After-School Programs.* Flint, MI: Author.

Muir, R. I. (1974). *An analysis of parent tutorial programs for children with reading disabilities.* Unpublished master's thesis, Brigham Young University.

Neuman, S. B. (1995). Reading together: A community-supported parent tutoring program. *Reading Teacher, 40*(2), 120-129.

Neuman, S. B. (1996). *Families reading together: Adult educational students and their preschool children.* Philadelphia: Temple University, College of Education.

Neuman, S. B. (1997). Guiding young children's participation in early literacy development: A family literacy program for adolescent mothers. *Early Child Development and Care, 217,* 119-129.

Neuman, S. B., & Gallagher, P. (1994). Joining together in literacy learning: Teenage mothers and children. *Reading Research Quarterly, 29*(4), 382-401.

Neuman, S. B., & Roskos, K. (1994). Bridging home and school with a culturally responsive approach. *Childhood Education, 70*(4), 210-214.

Neuman, S. B., & Roskos, K. (1997). Literacy knowledge in practice: Contexts of participation for young writers and readers. *Reading Research Quarterly, 32*(1), 10-32.

Nichols, T. M. (1992). A program for teachers and students: The Junior Great Books Program. *Gifted Child Today, 15*(5),50-51.

Nichols, T. M. (1993). *A study to determine the effects of the Junior Great Books Program on the interpretive reading skills development of gifted/able learner children.* Paper presented at the annual meeting of the Mid-South Educational Research Association, Knoxville, Tennessee.

Office of Juvenile Justice and Delinquency Prevention. (1999). *1999 National report series, juvenile justice bulletin: Violence after school* (NCJ 178257). Washington, DC: U.S. Department of Justice.

Olson, P. (1993). *Study skills across the curriculum.* Burnsville, MN: Reading Consulting.

Olson, P. (1995a). *Study skills across the curriculum.* Burnsville, MN: Reading Consulting.

Olson, P. (1995b). *Study skills across the curriculum: Impact evaluation study, grades 5-8.* Burnsville, MN: Reading Consulting.

Pederson, J., de Kanter, A., Bobo, L. M., Weinig, K., & Noeth, K. (1998). *Safe and smart: Making the after-school hours work for kids.* (ERIC Document Reproduction No. ED419303)

Piaget, J. (1952). *The language and thought of the child.* London: Routledge & Kegan Paul.

Piaget, J. (1964). *The moral judgment of the child.* New York: Free Press.

Pierce, K. M., Hamm, J. V., & Vandell, D. L. (1997). *Experiences in after-school programs and children's adjustment.* Madison: University of Wisconsin-Madison, Wisconsin Center for Education Research.

Pinnell, G. S. (1989). Reading recovery: Helping at-risk children learn to read. *Elementary School Journal, 90,* 161-182.

Pinnell, G. S., DeFord, D. E., & Lyons, C. A. (1988, April). *Sustained effects of a strategy-centered early intervention program in reading.* Paper presented at the annual meeting of the American Educational Research Association, New Orleans, Louisiana.

Pinnell, G., Lyons, C. A., DeFord, D. E., Bryk, A. S., & Seltzer, M. (1994). Comparing instructional models for the literacy education of high-risk first graders. *Reading Research Quarterly, 29,* 9-40.

Pinnell, G. S., Short, A. G., Lyons, C. A., & Young, P. (1986). *The Reading Recovery project in Columbus, OH, Year I: 1985-1986.* Columbus: Ohio State University.

Poinsett, A. (1996). *The role of sports in youth development: Report of meeting convened by Carnegie Corporation of New York.* New York: Carnegie Corporation of New York.

Posner, J. K., & Vandell, D. (1994). Low-income children's after-school care: Are there beneficial effects of after-school programs? *Child Development, 65*(2), 440-456.

Project Success Enrichment. (1995). *Proposal submitted to the Program Effectiveness Panel of the U.S. Department of Education.* Washington, DC: U.S. Department of Education.

Reid, E. M. (1989). *Exemplary center for reading instruction: Proposal submitted to the Program Effectiveness Panel of the U.S. Department of Education.* Washington, DC: U.S. Department of Education.

Riley, R. W. (1995). America goes back to school: From the desk of the Secretary of Education. *Teaching PreK-8, 26*(1), 6.

Riley, R. W. (1996). From the desk of the Secretary of Education. *Teaching PreK-8, 26*(8), 10.

Rosenthal, R., & Vandell, D. (1996). Quality of care at school-aged childcare programs: Regulatable features, observed experiences, child perspectives, and parent perspectives. *Child Development, 67*(5), 2434-2445.

Roskos, K., & Neuman, S. B. (1993). Access to print for children of poverty: Differential acts of adult mediation and literacy-enriched play settings on environmental and functional print tasks. *American Educational Research Journal, 30*, 95-122.

Ross, S. M., Smith, L. J., Casey, J., & Slavin, R. E. (1996). *Evaluation of the Extended Day Tutoring Program in Memphis City Schools* (Technical Report). Memphis, TN: University of Memphis Center for Research in Educational Policy.

Schlagal, R. C. (1989). Constancy and change in spelling development. *Reading Psychology, 10*(3), 207-232.

Schwartz, W. (1996). *A guide to choosing an after-school program. For parents/about parents.* New York: ERIC Clearinghouse on Urban Education. (ERIC Document Reproduction No. ED407448)

Seligson, M. (1986). Child care for the school-age child. *Phi Delta Kappan, 67*(9), 637-640.

Seligson, M. (1988). Finding the right after-school care for your child. *PTA Today, 13*(7), 13-14.

Seligson, M., & Allenson, M. (1993). *School-age child care: An action manual for the 90s and beyond* (2nd ed.). Wellesley, MA: Wellesley College, Center for Research on Women.

Shanahan, T., & Neuman, S. B. (1997). Conversations: Literacy research that makes a difference. *Reading Research Quarterly, 32*(2), 202-210.

Slavin, R. E., & Fashola, O. S. (1998). *Show me the evidence: Proven and promising programs for America's schools.* Thousand Oaks, CA: Sage.

Slavin, R. E., Karweit, N. L., & Madden, N. A. (Eds.). (1989). *Effective programs for students at risk.* Boston: Allyn & Bacon.

Slavin, R. E., Karweit, N. L., & Wasik, B. A. (1994). *Preventing early school failure: Research, policy, and practice.* Boston: Allyn & Bacon.

Slavin, R. E., & Madden, N. A. (1991). Modifying Chapter 1 program improvement guidelines to reward appropriate practices. *Education Evaluation and Policy Analysis, 13*(4), 369-379.

Slavin, R. E., Madden, N. A., Dolan, L. J., & Wasik, B. A. (1996). *Every child, every school: Success for all.* Newbury Park, CA: Corwin.

Steinberg, L. (1986). Latchkey children and susceptibility to peer pressure: An ecological analysis. *Developmental Psychology, 22*, 433-439.

Study Skills Across the Curriculum. (1991). *Proposal submitted to the Program Effectiveness Panel of the U.S. Department of Education.* Washington, DC: U.S. Department of Education.

Tierney, J., & Grossman, J. B. (with Resch, N. L.). (2000). *Making a difference: An impact study of Big Brothers/Big Sisters.* Philadelphia: Public/Private Ventures. Retrieved April 6, 2001, from the World Wide Web: www.ppv. org/indexfiles/sosindex.html

Topolovac, E. R. (1982a). *Jog America read-a-thon and TV viewing skills packet: Books and Beyond.* Sacramento, CA: California State Department of Education, Solana Beach Elementary School District.

Topolovac, E. R. (1982b). *Literature at home: Elementary/junior high Books and Beyond.* Sacramento, CA: California State Department of Education, Solana Beach Elementary School District.

U.S. Bureau of the Census. (1987). *After-school care of school-age children: December 1984* (Current Population Reports, Series P-23, No. 149). Washington, DC: Government Printing Office.

U.S. Department of Education. (1993). *National study of before- and after-school programs.* Washington, DC: Office of Policy and Planning. (ERIC Document Reproduction No. ED356043)

U.S. Department of Education. (1997) *Keeping schools open as community learning centers: Extending learning in a safe, drug-free environment before and after school.* Washington, DC: Author. (ERIC Document Reproduction No. ED 409659)

U.S. Department of Education. (1999). *National Household Education Survey.* Washington, DC: National Center for Education. (ERIC Document Reproduction No. ED417194)

U.S. National Education Commission on Time and Learning. (1992). *Summary: Second public hearing: The Extended School Program and its impact on the community.* (Southeast Regional Hearing, Murfreesboro, Tennessee). Washington, DC: Author. (ERIC Document Reproduction No. ED372484)

U.S. National Education Commission on Time and Learning. (1994). *Prisoners of time: Schools and programs making time work for students and teacher* (Report of the National Education Commission on Time and Learning). Washington, DC: Author. (ERIC Document Reproduction No. ED366115)

Vandell, D. L., & Corasaniti, M. A. (1988). The relation between third graders' after-school care and social, academic, and emotional functioning. *Child Development, 59*(4), 868-875.

Vandell, D., & Ramanan, J. (1991). Children of the National Longitudinal Survey of Youth: Choices in after-school care and child development. *Developmental Psychology, 27*(4), 637-643.

Vygotsky, L. S. (1978). *Mind in society: The development of higher mental process.* Cambridge, MA: Harvard University Press.

Wasik, B. A. (1997). *Volunteer tutoring programs. A review of research on achievement outcomes* (Report No. 14). Baltimore: Johns Hopkins University, Center for Research on the Education of Students Placed at Risk.

Wasik, B. A., & Slavin, R. E. (1993). Preventing early reading failure with one-to-one tutoring: A review of five programs. *Reading Research Quarterly, 28*(2), 178-200.

Wilbur, J. (1995). A gift of time: HOSTS: Help One Student To Succeed. *Partnerships in Education Journal, 9*(3), 1-5.

Will, H. (1986). Junior Great Books: Toward a broader definition of the more able learner. *G/C/T, 9*(1), 6-7.

Winocur, S. L. (1977). *A curriculum for choosing.* Newport Beach, CA: Newport-Mesa Unified School District.

Zigler, E., Finn-Stevenson, M., & Linkins, K. W. (1992). Meeting the needs of children and families with schools of the 21st century. *Yale Law and Policy Review, 10*(1), 69-81.

Zigler, E., & Muenchow, S. (1992). *Head Start: The inside story of America's most successful educational experiment.* New York: Basic Books.

Zigler, E., & Styfco, S. J. (Eds.). (1993). *Head Start and beyond: A national plan for extended childhood intervention..* New Haven, CT: Yale University Press.

Zigler, E., & Valentine, J. (Eds.). (1973). *Project Head Start: A legacy of the War on Poverty.* New York: Free Press.

Index

**CORWIN
PRESS**

The Corwin Press logo—a raven striding across an open book—represents the happy union of courage and learning. We are a professional-level publisher of books and journals for K-12 educators, and we are committed to creating and providing resources that embody these qualities. Corwin's motto is "Success for All Learners."